Kudos

"Jack Ewing's thirty-year adventure in a Costa Rican jungle has produced a book **full of infectious love and amazing lore.**"
— Daniel Quinn, award winning author of *Ishmael*

"I taught about leaf cutter ants to my sixth grade class and **the children were thrilled and amazed.** Your pieces on Baird's tapir were so good I simply read them to the class, out of which they decided to raise money to adopt a tapir. Thank you!"
— Stu Summer, middle school teacher - Hillsdale, New York

"Written in language accessible to everyone, the 32 stories in this book delve deep into the fascinating world of Costa Rica's tropical wildlife, skillfully intertwining ecological facts with current environmental and social issues which affect all of us. Even trained scientists will find something new in the personal, and often humorous, observations in these pages. **This book is perfect reading for every inquisitive traveler to Costa Rica.**"
— Rob Rachowiecki, author of *Lonely Planet Costa Rica* guidebook (the first five editions)

"Jack's essays offer **great insight into tropical natural history, rural Costa Rican culture and environmental issues.** The natural history is so well done and the environmental insights so painlessly integrated that I use the book in my tropical ecology and conservation course."
— Richard Andrus, Professor - Binghamton University, New York

"A fascinating collection of stories and essays from Jack Ewing's decades of observation of tropical flora and fauna. **This book is the fun way to learn about biological corridors and the interrelatedness of all creatures.**"
— Beatrice Blake, author of *The New Key to Costa Rica, 17th edition*

continued...

"*Monkeys are Made of Chocolate* is a tapestry of stories as rich as the land from which they came. Whether you like reading about huge snakes which always seem to come in pairs, the intelligent behavior of sloths, the ancient craft of boat building by digging out a tree trunk, or how toucans aren't quite as cute as they appear, this book is **a treasure trove of Costa Rican life and natural history.**"
— Georgie Wingfield, Agronomist - Sussex, England

"In this well-crafted selection of short stories, Jack conjures up the intricacies of the natural world as only one who has been deeply imbedded for decades can do. In the manner of a master storyteller, Jack Ewing mesmerizes us as he takes us on wonderful trips in and around the rainforest. **A must-read for anyone who has ever been in a rainforest, or is planning on visiting one.**"
— Excerpts from *Quepolandia*, a Costa Rican English monthly

"*Monkeys Are Made Of Chocolate* has served as the theme setter for numerous family discussions in our home-schooling family. Yes, the book is educational, but it is also **a thought-provoking adventure** into the questions that deal with some of the most basic and elusive issues confronting man today."
— Ben Vaughn, editor of Dominical.Biz

"The serious underlying theme of ecological consciousness and responsibility is attacked by Mr. Ewing with grace and a healthy dose of humor. Instead of preaching he shows us through real stories and highly imaginative characters the havoc that we are wreaking on our only Planet Earth."
— Jackie Spamer, *Dominical Days*, a Costa Rican monthly

Monkeys
are made of
Chocolate

Exotic and Unseen Costa Rica

Jack Ewing

PIXYJACK PRESS INC

MONKEYS ARE MADE OF CHOCOLATE: Exotic and Unseen Costa Rica

Copyright © 2005 by Jack Ewing

Published by PixyJack Press, Inc.
PO Box 149, Masonville, CO 80541 USA
www.PixyJackPress.com

First Edition 2005
Originally published in Costa Rica in 2003.

9 8 7 6 5 4

print ISBN 978-0-9658098-1-8
Kindle ISBN 978-1-936555-01-7
epub ISBN 978-1-936555-02-4

Library of Congress Cataloging-in-Publication Data
    Ewing, Jack, 1943-
    Monkeys are made of chocolate : exotic and unseen Costa Rica /
    Jack Ewing.-- 1st ed.
        p. cm.
    Includes bibliographical references.
    ISBN 0-9658098-1-1
    1. Natural history--Costa Rica. 2. Rain forest ecology--Costa Rica.
    3. Nature conservation. I. Title.

    QH108.C6E95 2005
    508.7286--dc22   2004028464

Printed in Canada.

Cover illustration by Jan Betts.
Interior illustrations by Georgie Wingfield and Diane Ewing.
Book design by LaVonne Ewing.

*To Steve Stroud
whose vision and generosity
have guaranteed Hacienda Barú
a secure future*

Map of Costa Rica

Contents

FOREWORD

When I'm before an audience, I'm almost always asked this question: Do I see any hope for the future of our endangered planet? My answer is yes, and I think this surprises many listeners, because they and I look for hopeful signs in different places. They look for hopeful signs in the tightening up of laws protecting the environment, in the rigorous enforcement of those laws, in the emergence of informed, dedicated legislators and political candidates, and they see nothing to encourage them in those places. Protective laws are weakened or unenforced, and one of the first environmentally-aware U.S. presidential candidates is defeated in favor of one eager to roll back environmental protections to further big-business interests.

The indicators I'm looking at are very different from these.

If there had been an Amazon.com to search forty years ago, it almost certainly would not have had a separate category for Environmental Conservation & Protection—and if it had, it would have listed a single book: Rachel Carson's *Silent Spring*. Today that category lists more than five thousand—and I'd be willing to bet that the vast majority of these were published within the past ten years.

What this signals to me is that a significant change in public awareness has taken place and is spreading very rapidly. This is the basis for my hope for the future. Change begins in changed minds. Changing minds has a domino effect, a cumulative effect that occurs when one event sets off a chain of similar or related events.

Jack Ewing's success in creating the Hacienda Barú National Wildlife Refuge is part of this growing domino effect—as is the book you're reading.

To make it clear how important this domino effect is, I'd like to give just one example of it in operation.

In 1994 the CEO of Interface, Incorporated—the industry leader of the commercial carpet business—read two books. One was Paul Hawken's *The Ecology of Commerce* and the other was my own *Ishmael*. Up to that time, this CEO, a man named Ray Anderson, had been very diligent about being in full compliance with all government regulations relevant to his business. But when he read these two books, he saw that being merely in compliance is not nearly enough. He made up his mind to do three things: first, to eliminate petroleum from his carpeting (and it had all been petroleum-based until then); second, to develop carpeting that can be 100% recycled—into materials from which all his new carpeting could be made; and third, to encourage his customers to think differently about their floor covering needs. Instead of buying carpet and discarding it when it's no longer serviceable, he will lease them carpet. When it's no longer serviceable, he'll take it back to be recycled totally and replace it with carpeting made from totally recycled materials.

My book and Paul Hawken's were dominos that tumbled into Ray Anderson, moving him to action. But Ray Anderson was a domino as well, and when he fell toward creating a truly sustainable business, his competitors were compelled to keep up in order to be competitive. (Thus Mr. Anderson transformed not only a single business but a whole industry.) Similarly, his suppliers—among them giants like DuPont—were compelled to start developing new materials and processes that would enable him to reach his goals. Within five years, Ray Anderson was recognized globally as a leading figure in the realm of sustainable development.

Paul Hawken and Ray Anderson both began their careers as entrepreneurs and ended up being famous as environmentalists.

Jack Ewing's career followed the same trajectory. When he first visited Costa Rica's Hacienda Barú in 1972, he was looking at it with the eyes of an entrepreneur, and what he saw was a cattle ranch and rice farm carved out of a coastal rain forest. He became a rancher and farmer. Paul Hawken's experience as a businessman gradually changed his vision of commerce. Jack Ewing's experience as a rancher and farmer gradually changed his vision of Hacienda Barú. By 1979 it no longer looked to him like a cattle ranch and rice farm carved out of a coastal rain forest; it now looked like a half-destroyed coastal rain forest.

Paul Hawken's changed mind prompted him to write a book. Ray Anderson's changed mind prompted him to reinvent his company. Jack Ewing's changed mind prompted him to turn Hacienda Barú into a wildlife refuge.

Such a work of restoration doesn't occur as quickly as a book is written, but by the turn of the century all traces of the farm and ranch had disappeared, and Hacienda Barú was once again a natural habitat, teeming with wildlife—world famous and officially designated as Hacienda Barú National Wildlife Refuge.

What gives me hope for the future of the world and the human race? It's Jack Ewing—and the fact that he belongs to a growing community of people with changed minds who are changing the world and the people around them.

To read *Monkeys Are Made of Chocolate* is to share in a small way the great adventure Jack Ewing undertook in transforming his part of the world. In fact, reading this book is an adventure in itself—rather like hiking through a jungle: you never know what you're going to stumble across next! I won't spoil your fun by listing the surprises ahead of you, but they're certainly there in multitudes—things you've never heard of, things you never even dreamed could exist or happen. There aren't many books that will tell you which phases of the moon are best for pruning trees, for castrating horses, and for cutting weeds—and convince you that this isn't just moonshine!

You'll learn from this book, you'll shed a few tears, and you'll have a lot of laughs. I certainly did.

— Daniel Quinn

PREFACE

In February 1972 I first visited a ranch called Hacienda Barú, located on the southern Pacific coast of Costa Rica. At that time about half of the land had been deforested and was being used for grazing cattle and growing rice. The other half, approximately 170 hectares (420 acres), was tropical rainforest, one of the few large forest reserves left in this part of the country. My wife, Diane, our four-year-old daughter, Natalie, and I had moved to Costa Rica in December of 1970. Our son, Chris, was born in San José in May 1972. Between 1976 and 1978 I worked full time at the hacienda, commuting weekly between there and San José. Then the whole family moved to Hacienda Barú. For eight years we lived without ordinary conveniences such as electricity, telephones and all-weather roads that many people consider to be basic necessities of life.

After having grown up in the typical, pampered lifestyle of upper-middle class America, the experience of living and raising a family in rural Costa Rica was sometimes trying, sometimes frustrating, usually fulfilling and never boring. The children thrived, Diane survived, and I found myself drawn ever deeper into the fascinating realm of tropical ecology while at the same time losing interest in livestock and farming.

The year 1979 marked the beginning of a long period of transition for Hacienda Barú. Thirty hectares of grazing land was retired as pasture and allowed to regenerate naturally into secondary forest. In the tropics, when you quit chopping the weeds, land quickly reverts to jungle. Today, ninety percent of the hacienda has been restored to natural habitat, and farming and ranching are no longer practiced. It has been given the official category of National Wildlife Refuge by the president of Costa Rica and has the same protected status as a national park. The refuge is known internationally and is visited by people from many different countries.

It was from these years of experience that I drew the substance for a series of essays that I began writing in the year 2000. These were published by several local English-language monthlies including *Quepolandia*, from Quepos; *PZ Guide*, from San Isidro; and the now defunct *Dominical Current*, formerly published in Dominical. *Monkeys Are Made of Chocolate* is a collection of thirty-two of those essays. They do not necessarily need to be read in order.

The tropical rain forest holds a fascinating story which is told through the interaction of its life forms. Ever tantalizing, its natural history is revealed only in bits and pieces, always full of surprises, begging you to look deeper. Discovering some new tidbit of sapience about the jungle doesn't bring you any closer to knowing all there is, but simply opens more doors, each unveiling its own enticing web of knowledge. In *Monkeys Are Made of Chocolate*, I give to you a portion of the reality I have acquired in more than thirty years of living in the jungle. It is my desire that in addition to being entertained, the reader will acquire a deeper appreciation for the natural marvels of planet Earth, and the millions of living organisms with which we share it.

— Jack Ewing
November 2004

Chapter 1

Monkeys Are Made of Chocolate

acienda Barú National Wildlife Refuge, a 330-hectare (815 acre) nature reserve, has more monkeys than people. It hasn't always been that way. When I first visited the Hacienda in 1972, it was a rice and cattle farm. I was there for two months before I saw my first monkey, a white-faced capuchin *(Cebus capucinus)*. The sight of the small, black primate with head and throat blanketed in white and accentuated by a shockingly human-like face still remains vividly imprinted on my mind. I had previously seen monkeys in zoos, but there is little similarity between wild and caged primates. It's like comparing prison inmates with free people working and playing together.

In the early 1970s Hacienda Barú had much more farm and pasture land and less natural habitat than it does today. There were three forests, one large and two small. These forested patches were all separated from one another by rice fields and cattle pasture. If a monkey wanted to go from one forest to another it would come to the ground and run across an open area, putting itself in danger from ground-based predators. Nevertheless, lack of food and other factors would often induce the monkeys to run this risk. There was neither enough habitat nor enough food in any one forest patch to support a large population.

Of the four monkey species in Costa Rica the white-faced capuchin is the only one that is omnivorous. I have seen them eat everything from flowers to lizards. Fruit is an important part of their diet, as are insects, geckos and just about anything they can catch and kill. Several of the Hacienda Barú staff have observed monkeys raiding bird nests and eating the eggs and hatchlings, and I know of two incidents when they killed and ate iguanas. But, mostly we see them eating fruit, seeds and flowers. They are very fond of cacao seeds, the basic material used in the manufacture of chocolate.

At least two species of wild cacao are found within the rainforest of Hacienda Barú, but the trees are few and scattered. In 1979 we planted about ten hectares of hybrid cacao for commercial purposes. We cared for the cacao and harvested it up until 1987 when, due to falling international markets, it ceased to be profitable. Then we abandoned the plantations. During the years when we actively worked the cacao the monkeys always stole a little from around the edges. After we quit, they moved in and took over, making cacao their major source of food.

About this same time Hacienda Barú began a program of regeneration of natural corridors between forested patches. The corridors sprung up rapidly with fast growing species of plants, many of which produce food for monkeys. All this extra food supply became available to the monkeys one to two years after the cacao did.

The cacao alone was an incredible nutritional windfall for the white-faced capuchins, whose only competitors for the cacao beans were the variegated squirrels *(Sciurus variegatoides)*. When monkeys eat cacao they rip a pod off the tree, bite through the thick outer shell, eat a mouthful or two and throw away the mostly uneaten fruit. Several days later, when the partially eaten pods begin to rot, the capuchins come to the ground to search for maggots within the abandoned shells. They stuff these fat, juicy fly larvae into their mouths with great relish. Of course, the half eaten cacao lying on the ground attracts lots of terrestrial mammals, like pacas, agouties and coatis, but the monkeys always seem to find plenty of maggots.

Prior to the windfall of cacao we had seen female monkeys with very young babies on their backs only in December. But, as with most primates, the white-faced capuchins are capable of breeding and bearing young at any time of year if they are healthy and well fed. Following the abrupt increase in food supply we began noticing a few females with newborn babies in June. A few years later, with the additional food and increased mobility provided by the wildlife corridors, we began seeing female capuchins with tiny young at any time of year. We were also seeing a lot more monkeys than ever before. Although we didn't actually do a census, it was obvious that the population was increasing.

In fact, this phenomenon applies to all living things, from hummingbirds to crayfish. All wild populations track their food supply. As food, whether that be field mice, sardines, mosquitoes, algae or cacao, becomes abundant the population of the feeder animal increases, and when the food supply diminishes so does the population of the feeder. When I was in school the professor used the classic example of coyote and jackrabbit populations to illustrate the point.

For those of you with analytical minds, what had happened with the capuchins and the cacao could be described in this manner: Start with a given mass of monkeys in a given area; let's say 300 kilograms (661 pounds) of monkeys on Hacienda Barú. If those monkeys must expend one calorie of bodily energy to acquire and consume one calorie of food, that mass of 300 kilos will remain constant. But, if they can acquire a calorie of food for less than a calorie of work, the total mass of monkeys will increase. Some of the increase will be in individual weight gain, some in longer lives, some in lower infant death rates and some from increased reproduction

3

and population. The lower the expenditure of energy, the higher the increase in mass. In short, if more, easily accessible food is available to them, there are going to be more, fatter, healthier and longer-lived monkeys.

Now, let's say someone clears all the land where the cacao and secondary forest have been providing extra food for the capuchins and then plants that land to rice, corn, soybeans or some other human food or builds houses or a hotel. In that case the monkey's food supply will decrease sharply, and the monkeys will have to spend more time and energy acquiring their basic nutrition. They will expend more than one calorie to acquire a calorie of food, and the total mass of monkeys will decrease. Some of this will be reflected in diminished population.

Now this concept is all very interesting, but it brings to mind a puzzling question. In 1950 there were only 2.7 billion human beings *(Homo sapiens)* on the earth. It took many thousands of years to reach that population level. Then, in the next fifty years, our population more than doubled to 6.1 billion people. Logic tells us that humans, with all our modern technology, have become extremely efficient at producing food. It would seem that we must be able to produce a calorie of food for only a fraction of a calorie of work. In reality, by the time we humans prepare land; plant and tend to our crops; manufacture and apply a myriad of agrochemicals; harvest, transport and process the crops; package and transport the food to the supermarket; take the food home and cook it and eat it, we have expended about ten calories of energy for every calorie of food we consume. How can this be?

For the answer I will refer to a videotape entitled *Food Production and Population Growth* with Daniel Quinn, author of the award winning book, *Ishmael,* and evolutionary biologist Alan Thornhill, Ph.D., Director, Learning and Communications, Conservation Science Division of The Nature Conservancy. In the video presentation Dr. Thornhill, referring to this quandary, tells us that,

"...the balance of the energy comes from fossil fuels. We supplement our diet with fossil fuels."

In other words, we are cheating ecologically. By utilizing fossil fuels we are able to appropriate the lion's share of the resources on the planet for our own use, thereby reducing those available to other living things. This would be the equivalent of some benevolent being stepping in and buying Purina Dog Chow® for the coyotes when the jackrabbit population gets too low.

The astronomical increase in human population and consumption of resources is creating a natural imbalance on our planet that precipitates many problems. These include global warming, the ozone hole, pollution, diminishing rainforests, melting ice caps and just about any other environmental problem you care to name. It is time we put some thought into doing something about the way we use the earth's resources. Our own survival as a species may depend on our solution.

So what can we as individuals do about this? I think we need to begin at home. We can do our share to correct errors of the past when, right in some of our own neighborhoods, vast natural areas were cleared of their natural flora and fauna and converted to the production of cattle and crops. We can take steps to restore much of this land to natural forest, thereby insuring that there will be ample habitat for other species such as monkeys, sloths, toucans, frogs, snakes and all the other millions of creatures that make up the biomass. In so doing we will create a healthier, better balanced environment for ourselves. The Path of the Tapir Biological Corridor (PTBC), a project of the Asociación de Amigos de la Naturaleza (ASANA), is taking positive action. The corridor will increase habitat and wildlife mobility by connecting islands of natural habitat along 60 kilometers (37 miles) of the Pacific coast south of Quepos *(see map on page 130)*. It will help people live in harmony with their environment.

Next time you are sitting in your favorite coffee shop drinking a cup of the finest Costa Rican coffee, spare a moment to reflect on what was necessary to produce your cup of coffee with milk and sugar. Lend a kind thought to all the millions of creatures that had to give up their existence when the land was cleared of jungle to plant the coffee trees and sugarcane and to provide pasture for the dairy cows that gave the milk. And when you bite into that chocolate donut, remember that monkeys are made of chocolate, but humans are made of fossil fuel, and there will probably still be cacao trees on this planet when the fossil fuels are all gone. ∽

Chapter 2

A Tale of Tzimin and Bolom

The old gold miner trudged up the nearly dry river bed, carbine in hand. The large three-toed tracks caught his attention. They came from the undergrowth on the left and advanced upstream, clearly outlined in the moist bottom. The footprints disappeared into a large clear pool spoiled only by a greenish-brown blob resembling horse manure floating on the surface. The tracks emerged on the other side of the pool, continued up the stream bed a short distance and entered a wallow. The muck in the middle was pressed flat. A confusion of prints and scuff marks were visible at the edge of the muddy depression. From there the three-toed tracks resumed their upstream course. The man followed for a short distance but stopped when he spotted the second set of tracks. These had four toes in the formation of a paw. Though smaller than the three-toed tracks, the paw prints were larger than the old man's gnarled and calloused hand. The gold miner hesitated and surveyed his surroundings. He gripped the carbine a little tighter and moved ahead. The second set of prints mingled with the first.

Abruptly the distance between paw prints increased; a few meters later the three-toed prints did the same. The man followed, acutely aware of his surroundings, finger near the trigger. Within

50 meters (164 feet) the paw prints disappeared into thin air, ceasing to exist. The trail of three-toed tracks continued on alone, still with ample distance between them but more deeply imprinted in the sand. A dark reddish brown splotch appeared beside the trail, then another and another. The distance between prints increased and the stains in the sand grew larger.

Just around the curve the old gold miner stopped dead in his tracks and raised the carbine. A large spotted cat lay on its side, head twisted back at an odd angle. Immediately in front of the motionless body, a log spanned the stream from bank to bank. The old man threw a stone that bounced off the large skull with a dull thud but didn't evoke the slightest twitch. The hunter relaxed slightly and moved deliberately forward. With his finger still on the trigger the old miner poked the motionless body with the barrel of the carbine, but there was no response. Bolom the jaguar was obviously dead. The man stared down at the magnificent beast and pondered the puzzling situation.

The larger three-toed tracks renewed their course, the distance between prints back to normal. The old miner ducked under the log and followed the trail up the dry stream. Scuff marks and knee prints were visible at one point. A few steps farther lay the owner of the tracks, bleeding, breathing with difficulty and flat on its side. The old miner withdrew his knife from the scabbard and slit the animal's throat, then sat down and watched it die. Tzimin the tapir was fat, well over 250 kilograms (551 pounds), with enough loin and round to feed the man and his two companions for a week. He thought about skinning the cat, but the sun was descending toward the horizon, and he already owned three jaguar pelts. Without the hide he could carry more meat. The old gold miner took all he could pack in his rucksack and left the rest for the scavengers. The miners would feast on the tenderloin that night and dry and salt the rest tomorrow...

Baird's tapir *(Tapirus bairdii)* was called *tzimin* by the Aztecs and Mayas and *tilba* by the Miskitos. In Mexico it is known as the *ante-burro*, in Belize the mountain cow, and in parts of Costa Rica the *macho de monte*. In Spanish the names *danta* or *tapir* and sometimes *anta* are used. Here in the south Pacific region of Costa Rica around Dominical, we call it the *danta*.

To some the tapir resembles a small cow and to others a large pig. As high at the shoulder as the waist of a tall man, with a mass equal to that of a couple of linemen from a Super Bowl team, this is Central America's biggest land mammal. Its head is large, with a nose that might be described as a sawed-off trunk or a lengthy upper lip. This prehensile snout is used for grasping the foliage that forms the tapir's diet and pulling it into his mouth. Each hoofed foot would cover a dinner plate. All four feet have three functional toes and the front feet each have a vestigial forth toe high on the outside. These digits are really hooves, and therefore the tapir is an ungulate, the only one in Central America with three toes. The tapir plays an important role as a seed disperser, consuming many seeds that pass through its digestive tract and are deposited into water with the feces. The water often carries the seeds far from their point of origin. The tapir is preyed on by the jaguar, puma and of course, man.

When humans first appeared in the Americas sometime between 35,000 and 10,000 years ago, many species of large mammals roamed these lands—creatures that now seem like legends. The hairy mastodons with their enormous tusks, the giant ground sloth that stood three times the height of a grown man, the giant bison, majestic animal of the plains, and the saber-toothed tiger all existed in ecological harmony for several million years. In a scant one or two thousand years humans eradicated all of these large mammals from the face of the planet. In Central America nothing larger than the tapir survived. With large populations that lived in extensive areas of inhospitable jungle and swamp, there weren't enough people to kill them all. Nevertheless the beeflike meat of *tzimin* supplemented the diets of the pre-Columbians and later of the Spanish colonists.

When the first modern-day settlers came to this region in the early 1900s *dantas* were abundant, but not for long. Both hunting and habitat destruction took their toll. By 1950 few were left. In 1955, Manuel Angel Sanchez was foreman of Hacienda Barú. That year, in the aftermath of a massive flood, he found the dead body of a *danta* on Barú beach, the first he had seen in over five years. Two years later he killed the last tapir anyone remembers seeing in this area. He shot it with a 28-gauge shotgun where it was wallowing in a mud hole located in the upper portion of Hacienda Barú. Antonio Hernandez of Hatillo thinks that tapirs still visited salt licks put out for his cattle in Dos Bocas as late as 1960, but he isn't sure of the date. Regardless of the exact date we can safely say that it has been over fifty years since substantial numbers of tapirs wandered freely through our region.

In 1983 Daniel H. Janzen Ph.D. wrote, in *Costa Rican Natural History*: "There are at least 20 to 50 (Baird's tapirs) in Santa Rosa National Park and probably 100 to 300 in Corcovado National Park." In his 1988 book, *National Parks of Costa Rica*, Mario Boza lists the Baird's tapir as being present in seven national parks and wildlife refuges on the Caribbean slope, Chirripó National Park and La Amistad International Park, which straddle the continental divide, and only Corcovado National Park on the Pacific slope. Additionally I know from personal contact with inhabitants of Los Santos Reserve to the north of our area that a few tapirs can still be found there. Even if there were 300 tapirs in each of these protected areas, a very optimistic estimate, there would be only around 3,000 tapirs in all of Costa Rica. The true figure is probably less than half that.

In recent years poaching pressure in many of these protected areas has been intense. Corcovado in particular has had major problems. The illegal slaughter is taking place in spite of the fact that Baird's tapir *(Tapirus bairdii)* is protected by the Costa Rican

Wildlife Protection Law #7317 and is listed as Endangered in Appendix I of the Convention on Trade in Endangered Species (CITES) international wildlife protection treaty. Unless the citizens and residents of Costa Rica do something drastic, and soon, to solve this problem, we may live to see the extinction of the country's largest mammal. We don't want the tapir to be a creature of legends for our grandchildren.

In 1994 a group of ASANA members drove over the Cerro de la Muerte to Santa Maria de Dota and hiked for ten hours across the Los Santos Reserve to a small village called Brujo. During the hike they were fortunate enough to see a tapir. For four years, ASANA had been talking to people about supporting a wildlife corridor project that would link all the remaining natural areas between the Osa Peninsula to the south and Los Santos Reserve to the north. The tapir sighting in Los Santos prompted the name "Path of the Tapir Biological Corridor," since tapirs are found at both ends of the corridor and once roamed freely over its entirety. We will know that the PTBC is a success the day we see tapirs wander through our region once again.

To help facilitate this, ASANA is working with local communities to educate the people about the urgent need to protect Costa Rica's natural heritage. Many communities are beginning to recognize the value of the forests, especially in relation to their water supplies, and the value of wildlife in relation to tourism, a big money earner. Through ASANA's environmental education program people are learning of the basic life sustaining services provided by the rainforest, such as the conversion of atmospheric carbon dioxide into wood fiber and oxygen. Groups of volunteer wildlife inspectors have been formed in many communities. People are starting to speak out against poaching. Thanks to everyone's commitment, the Path of the Tapir Biological Corridor has less poaching than Corcovado National Park. However there is still much work to be done and ways in which everyone, everywhere can get involved.

You can find out how to help by calling ASANA at 011 (506) 2787-0254 or visit *www.asanacr.org*.

...Tzimin moved cautiously out of the jungle, raising his head and long snout to sniff the light breeze. He moved slowly and deliberately out into the dry river bed. The scent of water wafted heavily in the air. Tzimin felt a heaviness in his gut. He followed his nose to the clear pool and barged in, splashing water with his large three-toed feet. Standing on the rocky bottom, Tzimin squatted slightly and expelled firm round globs of manure into the pool. The cool water felt good. A slight itchiness tickled his thick hide. He left the pool and continued up the stream. The soft-bottomed mud hole appeared on the shady side of the bank where past flood waters had eroded a hollow. Tzimin rushed in, plopped down in the middle and wallowed around in the sticky muck. It felt good on his skin, and, when dried, the caked mud would protect him from biting insects. Tzimin took his time and thoroughly enjoyed the mud bath. He eventually left the muddy depression and resumed walking.

The first inkling of danger came on the breeze. Tzimin quickened his pace and moved his large head nervously from side to side, nostrils probing the air. He started to run, but Bolom, the jaguar, was on him like a flash, the sharp claws tearing into his sides, the fangs digging into the thick hide on his neck. The adrenaline hit him with a jolt. Tzimin broke into a full run. The side of his neck near his throat burned with intense pain. Bolom bore heavy on his back, but Tzimin ran faster, even as the claws and teeth penetrated deeper into his body. Just around the curve he saw the large trunk across the stream. Tzimin summoned all of his reserve strength and headed for the log. Ducking his head, he lunged forward. The blow slowed his forward motion. He heard the snap of bone breaking and felt the relief as Bolom's weight left his back. Tzimin stumbled, fell to his knees, then quickly regained his feet. But the exertion, deep wounds and loss of blood were too much. Tzimin staggered up the stream a few more steps, stumbled again and fell to the ground. He made one feeble attempt to regain his feet without success, then yielded to fatigue and weakness. His body lay still on the stream bed. Tzimin was only vaguely aware of the old gold miner's machete as it sliced into his throat, quickly draining his life's blood.

The original version of this tale was related to me by an old gold miner I met near Caihuita in 1974. It supposedly took place on the Caribbean slope near Bri Bri sometime in the 1930s or 1940s. I read a similar story in a book called *Treasure Hunters*, but I no longer have a copy and don't remember the name of the author. I can't vouch for the validity of the tale, but I enjoy immensely the vision it evokes. ∾

Chapter 3
Raven Meets Toboba Tiznada

The itching came in waves, tickling and irritating to the point of distress. An involuntary ripple ran through her long slender body, and she changed position, trying to get comfortable. A vibration in the earth underneath alerted her senses—something big was moving around and not far away. The vibration increased in intensity as the large animal approached and passed nearby, then subsided and finally ceased. Relieved that the danger had passed, Toboba Tiznada returned her attention to the persistent itching. Again she moved her lithe body, rubbing against the root of the tree where she hid. Relief would be hours in coming as the old skin worked itself loose and separated from the new. It was always the same, and little could be done to speed up the process. She rested for a while and again flexed her muscles and rubbed against the hard wooden surface. The old skin slipped free from her head and then farther back on her neck. Maybe it wouldn't take so long.

After a time the vibration returned, slower this time and with less intensity. Toboba Tiznada shrunk back into her hiding spot and lay still, waiting. The animal was on the same path as the one that passed earlier but coming from the opposite direction. Then it hesitated and changed course. A wave of panic surged along her spine. It *was going to cross on her side of the tree right in front of her hiding place! She moved her head slightly to get a better look, but the loose skin partially covered her eyes, limiting her vision. The animal was much too big to eat, but it might harm her. Involuntarily her muscles tensed almost to the snapping point. The large animal moved in front of the root under which she was nestled, its shadow discernible through the dry flaky skin. Its body heat stimulated her sensors and, somewhere in her nervous system, a trigger snapped. Her head shot forward, mouth opened wide, fangs extended, until her nose hit the heat source. She bit down. One fang penetrated first the coarse fabric and then deep into the flesh and injected the liquid protein. The other fang was deflected as it went through the fabric and only scratched the skin of the large intruder. Muscle contractions quickly reversed, bringing her head back into the coil, then tensed again, ready for a second strike. Toboba Tiznada huddled back into the hollow and waited.*

Nancy Ravenfeld, known fondly as "Raven" to her friends, looked about her for the source of the sting. There were no wasps or bees buzzing around, but she could swear she had been stung. Thinking a nest must be under the massive buttress roots of the rainforest tree, she turned for a better look. Underneath the root lay the source of her "sting," a mature fer-de-lance viper *(Bothrops asper)*, about 1½ meters (5 feet) in length, with its body curled into a tight coil. In her five years in Costa Rica, Raven had only seen two other fer-de-lances, and neither of them was this light colored. A wave of terror hit as she realized what had happened. Raven's immediate reaction was to get away from the snake, which she did, scrambling back down the hill, until something inside her said, "Wait! I'm not supposed to run with a snake bite." She collected her wits and tried to figure out what to do.

The hike to the road through the farm would take too long. It seemed the best option was to cross the river to the palm plantation where she could hear workers' voices and trucks on the move. After being taken to the nearest village in a palm truck, hitching a ride that ended up in the ditch, hitching another ride and flagging down the ambulance on its way to meet her, Raven finally made it to the hospital, where a qualified team of medical personnel took charge of her treatment. She figures it was about an hour from the time she was bitten.

One fang penetrated her left calf and injected half the venom the fer-de-lance had intended. Fortunately, the other fang only passed through her denim pant leg and barely scratched the skin. One doctor began administering the antivenin intravenously, while another drew black lines on her leg as reference points for measuring the increase in swelling. If the leg swelled up too much they would have to split open the skin to relieve the pressure on the blood vessels. At one point violent trembling raked Ravens' entire body until her teeth clattered. The first night was miserable, but she felt much better by the next day. After seventeen days, she was released from the hospital. "They could have kept me longer," Raven recalled, "but I insisted." At home, she was an excellent patient, following her doctor's instructions to the letter. Her leg healed perfectly, leaving only a slight scar. Raven attributes her rapid and successful recovery to a combination of getting to the hospital quickly, excellent medical attention, the essential oils she used to

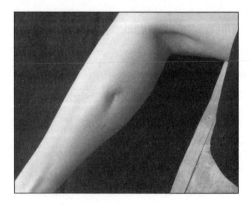

Nancy Ravenfeld's leg, three months after a *Terciopelo* snake bite. *Photo by Jack Ewing.*

treat the wound and the stroke of luck that only one of the *toboba tiznada's* fangs injected venom into her leg.

Snakebites are not a common occurrence in the jungles of Costa Rica. I live at Hacienda Barú National Wildlife Refuge on the southern Pacific coast, in the same region where Raven was walking that fateful day. I walk in the rainforest almost every day, and I usually see about half a dozen poisonous snakes annually. Most of those are fer-de-lances, commonly called the *terciopelo* in Spanish and occasionally the *toboba tiznada*. Over the years, I have seen several that made my hair curl. The biggest *terciopelo* I have seen on Hacienda Barú was a lone female. It was in September 1988 right after a three-day torrential rain. One of my workers killed her while she was trying to crawl to higher ground. We cut her open and found sixty-three eggs, each with a perfectly formed little serpent inside. I'm only 1.75 meters (5 feet, 9 inches) tall, but this monster was 2.32 meters (over 7½ feet) long and bigger in diameter than my thigh. Just looking at her sent a chill up my spine.

Chaperos are field workers who wield long machetes to chop weeds. They see more venomous snakes than anybody and know a lot about their habits. Serpents remain hidden from hikers and don't bite them because a person is too large for a snake to swallow and would be a waste of the precious venom. But a *chapero* swinging a machete, cutting weeds and brush, will disturb and frighten a snake, bringing it out into the open and causing it to try to escape or defend itself. *Chaperos* and other workers prefer not to kill snakes with a machete, because half a snake can still crawl and bite. However, due to the nature and circumstances of their work they often have no other choice.

Many years ago I worked at a large cattle ranch on the Caribbean side of Costa Rica. On several occasions different people, including myself, had seen a monstrous snake crossing the jeep trail at a particular location, but nobody had gotten a good enough look to identify the species with any certainty. Then one day it struck at a *chapero* named Pablo. He was chopping weeds near a fallen log, about 20 meters (66 feet) from the point where the big snake had been seen on the road. Bringing his arm back to swing his machete Pablo saw the raised head of the *terciopelo* an instant before it struck. As adrenaline shot into his blood stream, Pablo's knife-bearing arm swung forward with a speed and strength he didn't know he had, severing the head and a piece of neck as long as his forearm. As he swung, Pablo dodged to one side allowing the head to fly past him and tumble into the grass, lightly brushing his shirt as it went by. The severed head and neck turned and tried to bite his foot, but its momentum had carried it too far, and the short piece of neck wasn't long enough to crawl and propel the head nearer its target. As I came riding past on horseback five minutes later, Pablo hefted the huge reptile as high above his head as his arms could reach. A big piece of tail still lay on the ground, and the severed end was so thick that Pablo couldn't close the fingers of both his hands around it. When my horse attempted to sniff the poisonous reptile, the head curled around and nearly bit the horse's nose. That snake, the biggest viper I've ever seen, measured 2.78 meters (9 feet) long, and its head was so big I couldn't cover it with my open hand. Three days later one of Pablo's companions killed another *terciopelo* less than 5 meters (16½ feet) from the same log. This snake was a little smaller but still over two meters.

On that same ranch a *chapero* named Javier customarily wore a bandana wrapped and tied around his wrist on his machete-swinging arm. One day his crew of *chaperos* was chopping a pasture where several cattle had died from snake bite. Everyone was on high alert. Exactly like the incident with Pablo, a big *terciopelo* struck at Javier while he was swinging his machete, and just like Pablo, Javier severed its head. But the first *terciopelo* had a companion nearby, and it struck at Javier while his knife swinging arm was forward slicing through the first snake. The strike failed to penetrate Javier's flesh, but one of the fangs caught up in his bandana wrist wrap and squirted the venom uselessly into the air and onto his pant leg. Miraculously, the free fang never touched Javier's hand. Another *chapero* severed that second *terciopelo's* head a few seconds later. Both snakes were over two meters long. Incidentally, I worked at that ranch for six years, and, even though we had over seventy employees, nobody was bitten by a snake during that time.

In the early 1980s, when we still cultivated rice on Hacienda Barú, we had an interesting encounter with a two-meter-plus (over 6½-foot) *terciopelo*. Near harvest time, the mature grain heads attract lots of rats, and where there are rats there are snakes. On this occasion the large rice harvester was moving through the field cutting rice when one of the workers heard a thump... thump...thump against the metal fender. Suspecting mechanical trouble he looked toward the source of the thud. What he saw was a large snake flipping around with each revolution of the huge tire. The serpent had apparently been in the rice field and struck at the tire as the machine went past, driving its fangs into the rubber tread where they stuck tightly. The *terciopelo* was already dead, but it still unnerved everyone to know that it had been in the field where workers were walking around and loading rice sacks. Just the size of the serpent was enough to cause bad dreams. The next day a tractor was plowing the same field in preparation for planting a second crop, and it ran over and killed that serpent's companion, slightly larger than the first one.

When a *chapero* kills a large snake everyone in the crew hunts for the companion, because they know it's there and a danger to them all. If they don't find the second viper right away, they assume it is hiding and will turn up next time they chop that pasture, and it usually does. *Campesinos*, or country people, have learned how to live in the same habitat as poisonous snakes, and this is one bit of accumulated lore or local wisdom that helps prevent snakebite. The only two-meter-plus *terciopelo* I have seen that was alone, or at least its companion wasn't seen, was the egg-laden female displaced by the flood. All the others have been in pairs.

This may be true for other species as well. At Hacienda Barú we have had forest guards who patrol the jungle for the prevention of poaching since the late 1970s, even before the reserve became a National Wildlife Refuge. At that time I had yet to place restrictions on workers regarding the killing of poisonous snakes. I had enough trouble convincing them not to kill the nonpoisonous ones. In 1986 a forest guard named Gregorio saw a large black-headed bushmaster *(Lachesis meloncephala)*, known locally as the *plato negro*, which he killed with a stout stick. He wanted to bring the pit viper back for everyone see, but had work to do and wouldn't return past that particular spot for about five hours. Gregorio knew that a reptile's muscles will continue to contract for several hours after its death, so in order to ensure that his trophy would remain in the same place, he tied a small cord around its neck and tied the other end to a tree. Upon his return five hours later the "dead" snake was coiled up, head raised slightly in striking position, with its tail vibrating rapidly. He had to kill it again, and this time he made sure. The *plato negro* measured 2.2 meters (7¼ feet) in length. Five days later Gregorio killed a second bushmaster, exactly the same length, in the same location.

As illustrated by Gregorio's experience, the bushmaster is an extremely powerful serpent that can survive a beating. An old-timer I met in the Caribbean told me he wouldn't even consider trying to kill a large one if he was by himself, but instead would give it a wide berth. At the Instituto Clormiro Picado, where the antivenin for the treatment of snakebite is prepared, I have seen technicians handle these snakes and milk them to extract the venom. Two men can easily handle a two-meter *terciopelo*, but it takes three for a bushmaster. Additionally the bushmaster's venom is extremely potent for humans. Up until about fifteen years ago as many as three-quarters of all the victims of bushmaster bite died even when treated. However, the antivenin has improved as have the treatment procedures, and in recent years almost all snakebite victims have been saved.

Luis Montenegro is one of those who is thankful to the Instituto Clormiro Picado, for producing the excellent antivenin that saved his life when he was bitten by a black-headed bushmaster or *plato negro*. One night, when Luis and two companions were looking for freshwater shrimp for fish bait, the large pit viper struck. Both fangs penetrated the inside of his right ankle and injected their poison. Luis never saw the snake, but judging by the distance between the fang marks, the doctors later estimated that it was fully two meters (6½ feet) in length. Fortunately, the three men had a car nearby. They went first to the clinic in the village of Matapalo, about a thirty-minute drive, to look for a doctor and an injection of antivenin. In that short time, Luis's entire leg began hurting and blood seeped from the points where the fangs had pierced his skin. After a substantial delay, the three men determined that no help was available in Matapalo and proceeded on to the hospital in Quepos, where they arrived about two hours after Luis was bitten. The next morning he was transferred by airplane to the Hospital Mexico in San José. He remembers that the first doctor to look at his leg said they would most likely have to amputate. Luis remained in the Hospital Mexico for nine months, during which time he was taken to the operating room thirty times. With skin and muscle grafts, doctors rebuilt the tissue that was destroyed by the bushmaster's venom. Miraculously, they were able to save his leg.

When I interviewed Luis Montenegro six years later his right leg was much smaller than his left, and he walked with a pronounced limp. The inside of his ankle and calf was scarred and deformed. A gauze bandage was tied around the spot where the bushmaster's fangs had injected the venom. "Once or twice each month the old wound opens and pus oozes out," he told me. He has other scars on his thigh and calf where the doctors took tissue for the grafts. For over a year after his release from Hospital Mexico, Luis remained under treatment at the clinic in Matapalo. The photo of his leg and the open wound was taken at the clinic nine and a half months after he was bitten.

If all this scares you, then you have a normal, healthy fear of snakes. But it's good to keep things in perspective. These poisonous snakes expend a lot of bodily energy producing the venom that they inject into their victims. Once they inject it, several days will elapse before it is replaced, and during that time the snake can't eat, because it can't kill or digest its prey. That's the big reason why people are not in a high degree of danger from a venomous snake. The snake isn't crawling around out there looking for people to bite. If it were, many more bites would occur. I know of over one hundred incidences when people came within striking distance of a pit viper that didn't bite them. It has happened to me on many occasions. I often wonder how many times I have placed my foot a few centimeters from a large *terciopelo* and never knew it was there. The 1.6-meter (5¼-foot) serpent in the color photo *(see the color section of photos)* is one that we detected after a guide unwittingly placed his hand within a finger's length of its coiled form.

I've lived at Hacienda Barú National Wildlife Refuge since February 1972. During that time we've taken thousands of visitors on hikes through the rainforest and had scores of employees

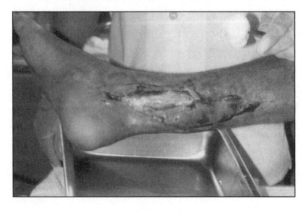

Luis Montenegro's leg nearly ten months after being bitten by a Bushmaster snake. *Photo by Jack Ewing.*

working in and around the jungle and, to date, we haven't had a single case of snakebite. A biologist with the Organization for Tropical Studies has calculated that field researchers with that institution worked in snake-inhabited tropical environments for over 450,000 person hours before anyone was bitten. That scientist happened to be the one who was out in the field at 450,001 hours.

There is some debate about the advisability and morality of killing poisonous snakes. Opinions range from people who think you should never kill anything to those who kill all snakes regardless of whether or not they are venomous. In the late 1980s when Hacienda Barú was in the midst of its transformation from cattle ranch and rice farm to biological reserve, I asked a biologist friend his opinion. He replied with a question: "How many snakes a year do you kill?" When I answered "eight to ten," he said: "Do whatever you think is best. Those few snakes on a reserve this size won't make any difference ecologically."

Another biologist friend, Jim Zook, once told me that he had an agreement with the poisonous snakes. "I leave them alone, and they leave me alone." In 1994 he was bitten by an eyelash viper in the Braulio Carrillo National Park, and during treatment had a severe reaction to the antivenin. Shortly thereafter, Jim told me that he had changed his mind and now would consider killing poisonous snakes, not because he hates them, but in his words: "I don't want anyone else to have to go through what I went through." Recently he told me that he takes more personal responsibility for avoiding venomous snakes by watching the rainforest floor more intently and wearing snake-proof chaps. He no longer trusts the snakes to keep their end of the "live and let live" bargain, but he doesn't kill them either.

Nancy Ravenfeld and Luis Montenegro do not hate the snakes that bit them either. Instead, they have come to understand that these poisonous reptiles live their lives in the only way they know how. The doctors told Raven that the snake that bit her was a *terciopelo*, yet she describes it as being much lighter colored than any of the photos I showed her. I suspect that it was shedding its skin. Pit vipers are said to be nervous and more likely to strike while shedding. As the skin breaks loose around the head, the snake is partially blinded and tends to strike at heat signals. This may have happened with Raven. Luis thinks he stepped on the tail of the *plato negro* that bit him, but he doesn't know for sure. The eyelash viper that bit Jim was lying on some foliage and bit him when he brushed it with his arm.

I haven't seen a two-meter-plus poisonous snake in over a dozen years. A herpetologist who was doing research at Hacienda Barú saw one in the spring of 2000. I know where two of them hang out, but I don't care to go looking for them. Since the entirety of Hacienda Barú is now a wildlife refuge, and we no longer have farmland or pasture, we don't have any *chaperos*, and for that reason probably see fewer venomous snakes. We've always had a policy of not killing nonpoisonous snakes; now we don't kill any of them. If a pit viper becomes a pest, we will remove it to a different location, but there have been few occasions when this was necessary. I'm sure the big ones are still out there, and they're certainly making babies. Maybe I'll get to see another one some day.

If you are thinking about a visit to Costa Rica and plan on doing a lot of hiking in the jungle while you're here, there are several simple measures you can take to minimize the risk of snakebite: (1) look in your boots before you put them on, (2) look before you step, and (3) buy a lottery ticket. Why buy a lottery ticket? Because in the short time you are in Costa Rica, you will have a better chance of winning the lottery jackpot than you will of getting bitten by a poisonous snake. ❧

Chapter 4

Eating the Seed Corn

One of the greatest environmentalists of all time, David Brower, former president of the Sierra Club, said in his book *Let the Mountains Talk, Let the Rivers Run*:

"In the years since the Industrial Revolution, we humans have been partying pretty hard. We've ransacked most of the Earth for resources. A small part of the world's population wound up with some nice goodies, but now we're eating the seed corn. We are living off the natural capital of the planet, the principal, and not the interest. The soil, the seas, the forests, the rivers, and the protective atmospheric cover—all are being depleted. It was a grand binge, but the hangover is now upon us, and it will soon be throbbing."

We're just beginning to feel the first symptoms of that hangover. We've all seen how weather patterns are changing. These days, when I visit my family in eastern Colorado during the summer, tornado warnings are commonplace. When I was growing up there a tornado warning was a rarity. It seems like every year the hurricanes get bigger and dissipate more slowly. The droughts and heat spells last longer and the winters are more severe. To complicate things even further, the polar caps are melting at an alarming rate and sea levels are rising. The best computer models can't accurately predict the weather for more than a couple of days, much less predict long-term weather events. Nevertheless, most researchers do agree that the situation has the potential for global disaster of monumental proportions. As Brower says, "the hangover is now upon us," and I say its name is global warming.

The only way to mitigate global warming is to reduce the greenhouse gases in the atmosphere. Of these, carbon dioxide is the most abundant. Reducing atmospheric carbon means cutting back on energy use or switching to cleaner sources of energy. Since the United Nations Conference on Environment and Development, held in Rio de Janeiro in June 1992, where the concept of making the polluters pay for the cleanup of atmospheric carbon was first proposed, the idea has been little more than talk for most of the world. But, while everyone else was procrastinating, tiny Costa Rica, with only a fraction of the earth's land area and population and no political clout, was taking action. But first let me explain exactly what I mean by making the polluters pay for the cleanup. The concept is sometimes called carbon credits.

Burning any hydrocarbon—like wood, coal, oil or gasoline—takes oxygen out of the air and puts carbon dioxide into it. Since there are close to one billion internal combustion vehicles in the world, 610 million of which are newer than 1990, they are a major source of atmospheric carbon. If you drive an average-size car, every time you burn a 15-gallon tank of gas you deposit 270 pounds of carbon dioxide in the atmosphere. Trees remove that carbon dioxide from the air and fix it in wood fiber, emitting oxygen in the process. Of course, we all breathe life-sustaining oxygen. So, the logic goes, those of us who drive cars should pay those who plant trees and protect forests.

In Costa Rica the program is called Environmental Service Payments. The way it works, in practice, is that people who purchase gasoline and diesel pay a special tax. The proceeds from that tax go to pay people who plant and protect forests. Since there isn't enough of the tax revenue to pay everyone who is conserving forest, some areas have priority over others. Wildlife corridors are one of the highest priority areas for the distribution of these incentives. The program has been operating since 1997. It is still small and has numerous problems, but it is working and has an incredible potential for protecting forest and restoring wildlife habitat. It is also an excellent example for the rest of the world.

Costa Rica has other programs that tend to mitigate carbon emissions. Here, as in most of the world, much of the electricity is generated at power plants that burn fossil fuels such as coal and diesel. This, of course, increases atmospheric carbon and reduces oxygen. Conservation in the use of electricity goes a long way to lower carbon emissions. With this in mind, the Costa Rican electrical utility, *Instituto Costarricense de Electricidad* (ICE), offers lower rates to customers who demonstrate that they are economizing. Stop and think about that. Those who are wasteful and consume large amounts of electrical power pay a higher rate per kilowatt hour than those who take measures to economize and use less. In other words there is no discount for volume purchases, but instead a penalty. The way you get a discount is by cutting down on your electrical consumption. Another thing that ICE does to encourage consumers to reduce their energy consumption is to promote the use of compact fluorescent bulbs. They even have special promotions when they sell these very efficient bulbs to clients at cost and finance them over a period of a year. You may think that the energy savings from switching to more efficient light bulbs is insignificant, but that's not the case. In 2001 when California was in an energy crunch, John Schaeffer, founder of Real Goods, calculated the savings that would occur if every household in the state were to exchange four incandescent 100-watt bulbs for four equivalent 27-watt compact fluorescent bulbs. The savings would not only be enough to eliminate the need for any new power plants, but would be sufficient to allow California to shut down seventeen average-size existing power plants.

Costa Rica isn't alone in its efforts to curtail carbon emissions. A few other countries are also doing their best to economize, and some are searching for cleaner forms of energy. The tiny country of Iceland is committed to becoming the first country in the world to be fossil fuel-free. They plan to completely eliminate fossil fuels by 2020 and replace them with clean-burning hydrogen and geothermal energy. Mexico is also looking into alternatives to fossil fuels in order to alleviate air pollution. China is doing likewise. Denmark, Holland and Germany are all investing heavily in alternative forms of energy such as wind power. Royal Dutch Shell, a petroleum giant, has also invested heavily in wind power. Many European countries have instituted high fuel taxes as an incentive for consumers to economize.

So what can you and I do? We can set examples in the way we live our lives. I never considered my brother Rex to be an environmentalist, but when I visited him in 2000, I was pleasantly surprised. Rex and his wife LaVonne live over 3 kilometers (2 miles) from the nearest electrical lines, yet they have all the modern conveniences of city dwellers. Their power comes from one small wind generator, an 1,140-watt solar array, twenty deep-cycle batteries and an inverter that makes the whole system 110 volts AC. That means they can plug ordinary appliances into their electrical outlets. But Rex and LaVonne's appliances aren't ordinary by any means; instead they are highly-efficient models. I was amazed and delighted to learn that all kinds of super-efficient appliances are available. Some will reduce electrical consumption as much as seventy-five percent compared to older appliances. Imagine the savings on a global scale if these efficient appliances were to come into general usage. With electrical energy the savings is even greater due to a multiplier effect. Inefficiency in the production and transportation of electrical power is such that it takes more than three watts of energy to put one watt of electrical power in your home. That means saving one watt of electricity in your home saves three or more watts at the power plant where your electricity was generated.

So here I am, thinking of myself as the great environmentalist, visiting my little brother, who never had any special inclination toward the environment, and learning a very important lesson from his example. Just think of what the readers of this book could do by example, even if the only action each of us takes is to change four incandescent light bulbs in our homes for four compact fluorescent bulbs and then tell everyone about it. I personally plan to go a lot further and convert my entire home to solar power. On those windy, rainy nights when a tree falls on the electrical lines and you guys are all sitting around in the dark trying to play cards by candlelight, I won't even know anything is wrong.

I also try to set an example by planting trees. No, I'm not really a tree hugger, but I do like trees and I do see some crucial reasons why we should be planting them, especially those of us who like to breathe. (1) Trees take carbon dioxide out of the atmosphere and convert it into wood fiber while at the same time releasing oxygen. (2) Trees conserve water, which is equally important to life. If we run out of water we will only live a little longer than if we run out of oxygen. (3) Trees, especially native species, provide habitat for wildlife. This is particularly beneficial when they are planted in corridors that connect isolated patches of forest. (4) Trees provide lumber, a valuable material that we use in our daily lives. (5) Trees provide paper, the usage of which the computer age has not only failed to eliminate, but instead, has multiplied. You can set a wonderful example by planting trees too.

As Brower implies in the quote at the beginning of this essay, we can't live off the natural capital forever. We need to come up with solutions that will enable us to begin living off the interest instead of the principal. Increasing our forest cover is one way to increase our natural capital and bring us closer to sustainable living.

Inform yourself and then inform others. There is a lot of excellent reading material out there for those who are interested in learning more. ❧

Chapter 5

Who Says You Can't Teach
An Old Sloth New Tricks

One of the craziest things I ever did was to climb a pochote tree so I could take a picture of a bird. If you've ever seen a pochote you'll know why I say that. It has long, thick, sturdy spikes about the size of your big toe. At Hacienda Barú National Wildlife Refuge, many of our guided tours pass through a pochote plantation, and curiosity about the spikes has prompted many of our visitors to ask why the pochote trees have such long spikes. The truth is that nobody really knows for sure, but there is one theory that seems to fill in the blanks and tie up all the loose ends. It was told to me by a young biologist, and I didn't think to ask him the source of his information. But right or wrong I think you will find the theory interesting.

Around ten million years ago North and South America were separate continents, each with its own peculiar flora and fauna. At that time the *Bombacaceae* family of trees, to which the present day pochote tree *(Bombacopsis quinatum)* belongs, was found only in North America. They didn't have spikes then, like they do today. That was about the time when volcanic activity and tectonic plate movements were combining forces to create the land mass which now connects these two large continents. That land bridge, of course, is called Central America. It is impossible to place an exact time when the connection was completed, because sea levels were not constant. According to Anthony G. Coates, editor of the book *Central America, A Natural and Cultural History*, beginning about three million years ago, the earth began to experience a regular cycle of ice ages approximately every 100,000 years. During each ice age much of the earth's water froze, tying it up in glaciers and the polar caps. This caused sea levels to drop. After each ice age the polar caps melted and sea levels rose again. The difference between the highest and lowest sea levels was 130 meters (426 feet) or more. Due to this variation the land bridge, in its early stages, wasn't always complete. During glacial periods when sea levels were low all sections of the bridge were above water and the land connection between the continents was complete. Then when the ice melted, sea levels rose, and water again covered the lowest sections of land bridge. Accordingly the migration of species between the two continents happened sporadically over a period of several million years.

According to S. David Webb, a contributor to the book *Central America, A Natural and Cultural History*, the first South American land mammals migrated to what is now Central America nearly eight million years ago, when the land bridge was probably no more than an archipelago of widely spaced islands. The first to swim the wide gaps were two kinds of large ground sloths, described by Webb as "bear-sized." One of these eventually extended its range as far north as Alaska and spread through all the regions of what is now the continental United States. There is no evidence of further mammal crossings until about five million years later. The rest of the ground sloths and tree sloths didn't begin arriving until about three million years ago, by which time the land bridge was looking more like a bridge and less like a string of islands. Today Central America still harbors two species of tree sloths, both of which are seen regularly on Hacienda Barú National Wildlife Refuge and in Manuel Antonio National Park.

The sloths of today are raccoon-size mammals that hang in trees, often beneath branches, and sleep a lot. They are categorized as folivores, meaning that they eat mostly foliage, or leaves. I have seen them eat the fruit of the strangler fig and the cecropia trees, but most of the time they eat only leaves. That's probably why they sleep so much. Leaves are high fiber and low energy and are quite difficult to digest. Sloths eat many different kinds of leaves, but they seem to have their favorites and will sometimes eat all the leaves off certain trees, leaving the branches denuded.

The pochote plantation at Hacienda Barú borders primary forest. We rarely see sloths in the pochote trees, presumably because of the spikes, but the boundary between the pochote and the natural forest is an excellent area to observe them. Both the three-toed sloth *(Bradypus variegatus)* and the two-toed sloth *(Choloepus*

hoffmanii) hang out in the unspiked branches of the rainforest trees at the edge of the pochote plantation. From their comfortable perches the sloths reach over, pull the pochote branches to their mouths and eat the leaves. Very seldom will

Looking down from the top of a spine-covered pochote tree. *Photo by Jack Ewing.*

one actually venture over onto the spiked branches. Nevertheless, the branches of a pochote aren't nearly as scary looking as the trunk, and it is possible for a very careful sloth to maneuver through them. It's tricky and they do it very gingerly, but there are occasions when we find sloths hanging, eating and sleeping in the spiked branches.

Some of the giant ground sloths that came from South America were 5 to 6 meters (16½ to 20 feet) tall, or about as high as the peak of the roof on a small single-story house in Costa Rica. Presumably the leaves of the trees from the *Bombacacae* family were as appetizing to sloths then as they are now. The theory goes that the ground sloths devastated the vast majority of the *Bombacacae* family, eliminating the young trees before they had time to mature and produce seed. The only individuals that managed to survive the onslaught were a few that had a rare gene that caused them to grow spikes on their bark. Those were the only trees that the sloths left alone and the only ones to flower, seed and pass on the genes for spiked bark. The individuals with the most and longest spikes were the most likely to survive and pass on their genes to future generations. In a relatively short time, perhaps 1000 years, the entire *Bombacaceae* family acquired the spiked characteristic in the young growing trees. Once the trees reach a diameter too thick for a sloth to climb, most of the spikes disappear. You can believe this theory or not. To me it seems reasonable.

The relationship between the sloth and the pochote didn't end with the appearance of spikes, but before I get into that, let me tell you a little more about the three-toed sloth. According to G. G. Montgomery in *Costa Rican Natural History*, baby sloths are weaned off milk at about six weeks of age and, from that time forward, eat only leaves. The infant's first taste of foliage comes at about two weeks of age when it begins to lick the green saliva that foams around edges of its mother's mouth while she is chewing leaves. I had the good fortune to see this once, at very close range, while climbing in the crown of a giant rainforest tree at Hacienda

Barú. Even though the baby sloth quits nursing at six weeks, it stays with its mother for another four and a half months, after which time it is weaned socially. In other words it goes one way and mom goes the other. In practice, however, it isn't quite that simple. Weaning time is very traumatic for the juvenile, and once the mother decides it is time to make the break, she needs to figure out how she is going to ditch junior. Outrunning him is hard work.

Every year the spiked pochote trees lose all their leaves around the beginning of December. They remain bare branched until April when the rains resume. In the interim they flower and produce a seed pod which opens and sends the pochote seeds floating on the wind in puffs of cotton. Social weaning time for three-toed sloths comes along about the time the trees are putting on tender new leaves. At the same time we often find weaning-age sloths in the pochote branches as far as 30 meters (98 feet) into the plantation. For the first two years we observed only one, then a second one appeared. In 2001, the fifth year, there were three. One day while guiding a group of visitors, we saw a mother sloth with her large male off-spring about 20 meters (66 feet) into the pochote plantation. A couple of hours later when we returned on the same trail, the youngster was alone at the spot where we had seen both ear-lier, and the mother was almost back to the rainforest. The weanling, being much less adept at moving through the

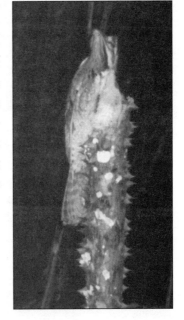

A Common Potoo bird with a 3-day old chick, resting on top of a pochote tree. *Photo by Jack Ewing.*

tree tops, took a week to work his way out on the spiky branches. In the meantime he had plenty of tender young pochote leaves for nourishment. When he finally made it to the rainforest, mom was long gone. For about two weeks junior hung in the tree where he had last been before his mother took him into the pochote and abandoned him. Finally the youngster began to venture out and explore his surroundings. It appears that one female figured out this weaning strategy and later at least two more started using the same strategy. Whether each mother figured it out for herself or the first one taught the other two is a mystery.

Sloths are learning other ways to exploit the pochote, but first a little more background. Back in the early 1970s, when Hacienda Barú was a cattle ranch and rice farm, there were only three forested areas in the coastal lowlands. All three were surrounded by deforested land. Over the years we created natural corridors to allow wildlife to move freely between these forest fragments. By the mid-1990s all of the forested areas on Hacienda Barú were connected to one another. None remained isolated, and the increased movement of wildlife was amazing. I first saw a sloth in the lowlands in 1996. Today they are a common sight along the corridors and in all the forested areas.

Near our house in the lowlands, my wife, Diane, has some horses with enough pasture for them to graze. The fences are lined with pochote interspersed with other tree species, and lines of pochotes cross the pastures in many places. One day while walking over to the office I spotted an adult female three-toed sloth hanging in the spiky, leafless branches of a pochote tree, the third pochote in that line. It was such an unusual sight that I called the Hacienda Barú naturalist guides to come and see it. Most seemed to think that it had come to the edge of the secondary forest and continued on, looking for more food and mistakenly followed the line of bare branched pochotes in hopes of finding better foliage farther down. But that sloth hung around for more than a week. We saw it almost every day and always in a pochote. There were other species of trees nearby, ones without spikes. Obviously this sloth was either a masochist, or there was more to the situation than we were observing. Then one afternoon I saw the familiar sloth in a pochote tree about 200 meters (656 feet) from its original appearance. This time I had my spotting scope and quickly focused it on the sloth. She was eating the pochote flowers and newly formed seed pods. We named her flower girl. She had learned what the squirrels and birds figured out years ago: Pochote flowers and pods are very tasty, so much so that it is worth learning to navigate an obstacle course in order to get them. Who says you can't teach an old sloth new tricks.

When you take into consideration that prior to 1985 there were no pochote trees anywhere in this area, these two new aspects of sloth behavior become even more interesting. Pochote grows naturally in Guanacaste Province, but all the pochote in our area was brought here in the last twenty years. By planting it at Hacienda Barú National Wildlife Refuge in places where sloths could get to it, we unwittingly set the stage for the sloths to demonstrate their innovative talents. In other words, they learned a couple of new tricks. I guess you could say the sloths have a love-hate relationship with the pochote: love those leaves, flowers and pods, but hate those spikes. And, from the pochote's point of view: hate those sloths. ᦉ

Chapter 6

There's a Fungus Among Us

About thirty years ago Diane and the kids lived in an apartment in San José, and I traveled back and forth between there and Hacienda Barú each week. The guy who lived in the apartment upstairs was a mycologist. That's a fancy word for someone who knows everything about fungus. Jesse was his name and he grew mushrooms for a living. He used to bring home bags of fat, juicy mushrooms and share them with all the neighbors. Since I love mushrooms about any way you can prepare them, I have always retained a pleasant memory of Jesse. Before making his acquaintance it never occurred to me that it might be difficult to grow them. After all, mushrooms are just a fungus and this is a hot, humid climate where fungus goes wild. It grows really well in places where you don't want it, like on bread, fruit, binocular and camera lenses, VHS tapes, and between my toes. You can't get rid of the stuff. Growing it is easy; keeping it under control is the problem. Anyway, that's what I thought. But Jesse told a different story.

I can't remember all the details because it was a long time ago and the process was very complex. The mushrooms were grown in hothouses where temperature, humidity and ventilation were carefully controlled. This was in the 1970s before the computer age, but for that time, the equipment he used to control the environment around the mushrooms was very sophisticated. The medium where they were grown was cow manure that was specially prepared and tested to make sure that the pH was correct and that it wasn't contaminated with bacteria or other types of fungus. Minerals and other nutrients were added. Contamination was the most serious problem. I remember a time when Jesse's mushrooms had become infected with something or other. He was a nervous wreck, getting up in the middle of the night to go out and check on the mushrooms and generally driving his wife crazy. He was like a mother with a sick baby, but his baby was a fungus. Growing mushrooms was far from being the piece of cake I had imagined.

Living near the rainforest and learning its secrets tends to change the way you look at things. One of my major learning experiences with regard to nature's wonders was when I discovered ants that cultivate fungus for food. You may know them as parasol ants or leaf-cutting ants. They have been doing what Jesse does for around fifty million years and they do it with only the tools provided by Mother Nature.

Atta cephalotes is the most common species of fungus-growing ants in this part of the tropics, but there are close to 200 species throughout the Americas. With a very elaborate social structure and communication system the *Atta* ants are considered to be one of the most highly evolved of the fungus growers. Daily they accomplish feats that are almost beyond human comprehension. So, let's have a closer look.

Leaf-cutting ants harvest more foliage than any other group of animals in the neotropics. They utilize around fifteen percent of all the green matter produced by the rainforest. A large colony of seven or eight million ants will consume as much green matter as a cow, but much of this foliage is not eaten directly by the ants. They do consume some of the plant juices, but the more fibrous parts of the leaves are fed to a fungus, which breaks it down into more basic nutrients. The ants then eat the fungus, which is their primary food source. Only one kind of fungus will work for them, and DNA testing has determined that the fungus the ants grow today is genetically identical to the one their ancestors cultivated fifty million years ago when these early agriculturists began developing their skills. They have kept it pure by not allowing it to fruit and propagating it only by cloning.

Many of us have seen green columns of leaf-bearing ants marching through the forest, across our lawns, or through our gardens. Some of us have followed those trails and found that it is not unusual for the leaf cutters to walk as far as two city blocks, climb to the top of a tree as tall as a ten-story building, cut pieces of leaves and flowers and carry them all the way back to their colony. Unfortunately, some of us have also learned that leaf cutters have a special affinity for anything new that we plant in our gardens. If we plant something that is not native to Costa Rica they will usually strip it of all foliage in a very short time. A few of us who simply must investigate further have noticed that, although most of the ants appear to be about the same size and shape, there are a few that are much larger than the leaf carriers, while others are much smaller and often ride on the leaf crescents being carried by their sisters. To learn more about these fascinating creatures, we must have a look into the writings of those who have delved deeper into the world of *Atta cephalotes*. I owe much of my knowledge about the fungus growers and the information I share with you here to the extensive writings of E. O. Wilson, Bert Hölldobler, Erich Hoyt and G.C. Stevens.

In order to deal with the problems of cultivating their particular kind of fungus, *Atta cephalotes* have evolved their own complex system. You could say that the ants bring the fungus into their homes. They build an underground colony which, on the average, consists of about 1,500 chambers connected to one another by tunnels. The smallest chambers are the size of your big toe and the largest the size of your head. Some are used for living and resting quarters, some for waste disposal, some for brood production, one is for the queen and others are for fungus production. Ideal levels of temperature and humidity must exist in the fungus production chambers. To accomplish these objectives and fulfill their needs, the ants build their city in a very specific way.

An average leaf-cutter colony with approximately five million ants is from 3 to 6 meters (10 to 20 feet) deep. Digging and moving the amount of earth necessary to create such a colony is a colossal task comparable to the building of the pyramids in ancient Egypt. One researcher measured and weighed the dirt that the ants had excavated and piled into a mound on top of their average-size colony. The leaf-cutter ants had, over a period of about five years, carried to the surface 22 cubic meters (29 cubic yards) of earth weighing over 30 tons—about two large dump truck loads.

The shaft exits in the mound are always situated so that rain will drain away from the openings. The principal ant entrances are located away from the mound of dirt, usually lower. In order to create air flow and control the humidity and temperature, the ants pile all their refuse, including dead ant bodies, unused leaves and other useless organic matter, in large chambers near the bottom of the city. As it decomposes, this material heats up and raises the temperature of the surrounding air, which then rises through the labyrinth of tunnels leading to the top of the mound. The rising air creates a draft which draws in fresh air from over 1,000 vents. The temperature and humidity of the chambers will vary according to their distance from the hot air flow. The fungus is cultivated in chambers which are located where optimum conditions exist.

The basic growth medium used in Jesse's mushroom operation was specially prepared cow manure. In *Atta cephalotes* colonies, leaf matter is the basic medium for fungal growth. Its selection, preparation and care is a meticulous process which if done properly will result in lots of good healthy fungus. Finding the proper leaves is the first step. The selection process is poorly understood by anyone but the ants. Nevertheless it is known that the colony sends out scouts to search for suitable leaf material. Any plant species new to the colony must be tested before any quantity of its leaves are brought into the fungus cultivation areas. A single scout discovers a plant that is unknown to the colony. She cuts a piece of leaf and returns with the fragment, leaving chemical markers along her path. She delivers the fragment to another worker within the colony. That worker prepares the test leaf, being careful to keep it separate from the rest of the fungus-growing medium. She then places some fungus on it and monitors the results. If the fungus thrives on the new material a crew of several thousand leaf carriers are dispatched out into the jungle to the exact location where the original leaf fragment was collected. There they cut and transport substantial quantities of the new foliage to the nest.

Think about the magnitude of this undertaking and the communication skills that come into play. It could be compared to a person going into a city with a population in excess of five million and delivering a single document to a government office. Imagine that this messenger leaves the document with one employee out of the many thousands who work there. That employee immediately begins a study of the document in order to verify its validity. After two days, it is determined that the document is authentic, and several thousand other employees are dispatched to a distant location which is encoded into the document. They go directly to the correct place located some 10 to 15 kilometers (over 9 miles) from the government office. Then they perform some action that will be beneficial to everyone who lives in the city. I have trouble imagining this scenario happening with any human government, but the leaf-cutters do it all the time.

All the members of the colony contribute directly or indirectly to the cultivation of the fungus. The most obvious of the seven distinct castes of *Atta cephalotes* are the leaf carriers marching through the forest with their green parasol-like cargo. When they arrive at the colony and deposit their leaf crescents, another caste takes over: the cleaners. Each leaf fragment is meticulously scraped and licked until clean. Later it is cut into smaller pieces, chewed, mixed with saliva and formed into a soft wad. The ants then place some fungus starter material, called mycelia, on the medium and place it beside other newly planted fungus in a suitable chamber.

From that point another caste, the fungus caretakers, step in and take over the process. These ants are responsible for keeping the fungus clean and free from impurities and infection. They do this partially by physically removing any foreign life form that tries to grow on either the medium or the bread-like fungus. But they have a few other tricks up their sleeves. A recent article in the *New York Times* entitled "Ants, Mushrooms and Mold: An Evolutionary Arms Race" by Nicholas Wade, tells us that the leaf-cutter fungus has long been plagued by a mold that is capable of wiping out the entire food supply of the colony in just a couple of days. However, the ants have an ally who helps them combat this enemy. A bacterium that lives in a patch on the ant's skin produces an antibiotic that controls the mold. In Wade's words, referring to the leaf-cutters: "They developed two remarkable inventions—agriculture and antibiotics—some fifty million years before people did. Beyond that, they have learned how to handle technologies more skillfully than the bumbling civilization above their heads. They can grow a monoculture—a genetically homogeneous crop, something that in human hands generally leads to disasters like the Irish potato famine—and they have also learned how to deploy an antibiotic without the target pest's becoming resistant to it."

So next time you have a delicious mushroom sauce or salad with your dinner, spare a moment to pay silent tribute to *Atta cephalotes*, the leaf-cutting ants. In these short pages I have only scratched the surface of describing the lives of these fascinating creatures. Volumes have been written about them. One such book that is very readable for nonscientists like you and me is *The Earth Dwellers* by Erich Hoyt. It reads like a best-selling novel. ∾

Chapter 7

Everybody Loves Toucan Sam...or Do They?

uiding visitors on ecological tours can be very rewarding. Showing guests their first monkey, sloth or toucan is as gratifying for the guide as it is for the visitor. Birds and animals aren't usually obvious to the untrained eye, and it is often difficult to explain or point out to people the exact position of wildlife within the dense vegetation of the rainforest. A typical conversation might go something like this: "See him? He's right over there." *"Right over where?"* "Look, just follow that trunk up to where it forks off to the left..." *"Wait a minute, which trunk?"* "That big one just to the right of the one with the vine." *"Oh yeah, that one. Okay now, I follow that up to the fork, right? Then where?"* And so on, and so on. Once the bird or animal has been spotted with the naked eye, the next step is to find it with binoculars. Some visitors are practiced in the use of optical equipment, but many are not, and it is sometimes difficult for them to locate the wildlife. I have noticed that visitors will sometimes say they see something even if they don't. However, there is never any doubt when the person encounters their first toucan. When the large yellow, black and red bird with the enormous beak comes into their field of vision, the visitor's reaction can range from a simple, *"Oh, my god,"* to a high-pitched squeal. Nowadays all of our guides have telescopes which they can quickly focus on the wildlife, eliminating all the inconveniences and getting right down to the nitty-gritty.

Everybody loves toucans. I'm relatively certain that the toucan has lent its name and image to more Costa Rican tourism businesses than any other bird or animal. Even outside of Costa Rica a popular breakfast cereal is identified with the famous Toucan Sam™ the Froot Loop™ bird. I use the word toucan here in the generic sense, but in reality there are many different kinds of these charismatic birds with their long boat-shaped beaks.

Costa Rica boasts six different species of toucan, two of which are found in the region around Dominical. The larger of these two, the chestnut-mandibled toucan *(Ramphastos swansonii)*, known locally as the *quioro*, is the largest toucan in Costa Rica. It is about the size of a small chicken. This impressive bird is mostly black with a yellow bib, chestnut on the lower portion of the bill and yellow on the upper. When seen from underneath a patch of red is clearly visible under the tail. A visitor once remarked to me that it should be called the "red-butted toucan." The smaller toucan found in this area is called the fiery-billed aracari *(Pteroglossus frantzii)*. Known locally as the *cusinga*, this beautiful bird has lots of red and yellow on the beak and body. At about 250 grams (9 ounces), the *cusinga* is only about one-third as heavy as the *quioro*.

The call of the *quioro* sounds like the Spanish words *"Dios te de,"* repeated over and over, and it is therefore known by that name in some parts of Costa Rica. A couple of years ago, a very observant Hacienda Barú guest named Vicki figured out what the toucans communicate to each other when they repeatedly emit these melodic notes. Being an avid naturalist, Vicki was invariably up early and out on the trails with her binoculars. One morning she observed a group of eight chestnut-mandibled toucans flying across a sparsely wooded area. She watched while the group made their way to a fruit-bearing strangler fig tree about 300 meters (984 feet) away. They traversed that distance in four short flights. On each leg of the journey the leader of the group flew about 75 meters (246 feet), landed in a tree and promptly began calling, *"Dios te de, Dios te de, Dios te de."* One at a time the other seven toucans flew to the call, and each landed in the same tree as the leader. When the last toucan arrived, the leader immediately stopped calling and flew away on the next short flight. When the leader reached the location of the heavily fruited strangler fig, it landed in an adjacent tree and repeated the calling routine. Once all of the toucans had arrived, the entire group silently followed the leader over to the fig tree and started eating. Somehow the lead toucan was able to determine when the last member of the group had arrived. Whether it made this judgment by counting the arrivals, by recognizing the last toucan as an individual, or by some other method, is anybody's guess. In any case, when the toucan calls, it is obviously saying, *"I'm over here, I'm over here, I'm over here."* Listen carefully next time you hear one and see if you don't agree.

My wife once bought me a fiery-billed aracari for my birthday. Diane and I both love animals, but we disagree about keeping birds for pets. She likes to have them around the house, and I prefer to see them out in the jungle. Nevertheless, after a couple of weeks of cleaning the toucan's cage, Diane reluctantly agreed that some things are best left in the wild. We decided that the famous "Froot Loop™ Bird" should more appropriately be called the "Fruit Poop Bird." The fruit just goes in one end and comes out the other. We released the beautiful *cusinga* into the wild where it could use its fruit-pooping ability as a natural mechanism for dispersing seeds across the countryside, thus performing a valuable service for the environment by helping to restore forest in areas where the natural cover has been lost.

It is a miracle that chestnut-mandibled toucans can even fly. That enormous beak sticking out in front causes them to fly in a position that looks like they're about to take a nose dive. Toucans normally land on the lower limbs of a tree and hop up from branch to branch, taking off again near the top. They use this strategy to gain altitude, since it is extremely difficult for them to ascend while flying. The beginning of a typical flight pattern is a dive, which is probably necessary to pick up enough speed to remain airborne. Next, the large black and yellow birds level off for the middle portion of the flight. Landing is preceded by an abrupt ascent or flaring, which slows and then halts forward motion. Most chestnut-mandibled toucan flights are short, less than 100 meters (328 feet).

If toucans are the lumbering old transport planes of the bird world, then the swifts, swallows and martins are the fighter jets, and the flycatchers are the stunt planes. Flycatchers are a large and diverse family of which thirty-eight different species have been identified on Hacienda Barú National Wildlife Refuge. I have always marveled that these relatively small birds can attack large birds of prey such as hawks and falcons and get away with it. A flycatcher is so agile that it can fly off a perch in a horizontal line, grab an insect in midair and turn around and fly back to the perch without dropping an inch. The flycatcher would obviously have to stop in midair to accomplish this feat. I am convinced that it must be an optical illusion, but I have seen this happen many times and it never fails to amaze me.

With all of this in mind, you can imagine how I felt the first time I saw a pair of flycatchers called great kiskadees *(Pitangus sulphuratus)* dive-bombing a chestnut-mandibled toucan. To my way of thinking the poor, beautiful, awkward, inoffensive fruit-eater was being unmercifully attacked by a terrorist squad of daredevils. However, in nature, as in human affairs, things are never quite as simple as they first appear. A year later I had the opportunity to witness the other side of the story. One day while driving down the road I caught sight of a toucan flying toward the jungle from across a clearing. I had grown accustomed to seeing the harassment of these beautiful birds by various species of flycatchers, and I wasn't surprised to see a pair of kiskadees attacking. As the birds approached, I noticed that the kiskadees' aggressive behavior was inordinately desperate and frenzied. Then, to my horror, I saw why. My poor, beautiful, awkward, inoffensive fruit eating toucan had turned into a baby-killer. It was carrying two kiskadee nestlings in its boat-shaped bill. One was severely mangled and probably dead, and the other was badly maimed but still alive and struggling. That incident was truly the beginning of my education into the harsh realities of nature. Another incident that took place several years later but with different actors served to further develop my understanding of the brutal natural pressures endured by wildlife.

The lineated woodpecker *(Dryocopus lineatus)* is an exceptionally beautiful bird that looks like Woody Woodpecker. One of our guides at Hacienda Barú National Wildlife Refuge once noticed that a pair of them were pecking away at a dead tree trunk close to one of the trails. It took about a week for the woodpeckers to hollow out an adequate nesting cavity. Next the female laid her eggs, and both took turns incubating them. Soon thereafter a pair of chestnut-mandibled toucans started hanging around the tree. They harassed the pair of woodpeckers for two days until finally one of the toucans managed to stick its bill into the hole and grab the woodpecker that was sitting on the nest. That toucan dragged the woodpecker out of the nest by its big red head. Then the other one grabbed the woodpecker's feet, and the two of them worked together, repeatedly bashing the woodpecker against the tree trunk until it quit resisting. They threw it on the ground and turned their attention to the nesting cavity. After eating the eggs one of the large toucans squeezed inside the hole and tried it out for size. A Hacienda Barú guide recovered the badly bruised and mangled woodpecker, but it died within a few hours. The next day, the pair of toucans apparently decided that the cavity didn't meet their requirements and abandoned it. A month later a pair of fiery-billed aracaris tried out the nesting cavity, but they abandoned it after three days. In human terms, this event is tantamount to a squatter killing the owner of a newly constructed home and stealing the house, only to abandon it a day later because it didn't meet his expectations.

I still love toucans, but I no longer have any illusions about who is good and who is bad in nature. From the moment that I saw the baby flycatchers in that toucan's bill my whole fantasy about relationships in nature came tumbling down. Everything became crystal clear. There are no villains nor victims nor good nor bad. Everything simply is. Every living thing has to eat, and that's what life is all about. Sooner or later we all go back to the earth and the nutrients get used again by another life form. Dead matter gets broken down by the predators, scavengers, insects, worms, bacteria, molds and fungi, and the basic components are restructured by the plants, thus continuing the cycle. That, my friends, is the story of life on this earth. We all came from the earth, and we all return to it, fueling the continuous cycle of life. Nothing escapes, not animal nor plant nor even mineral. It is all part of this planet. You can think of the earth as a living, functioning organism, a marvelous recycling center that recycles everything from fallen trees to dead woodpeckers, because that's what it really is. ∽

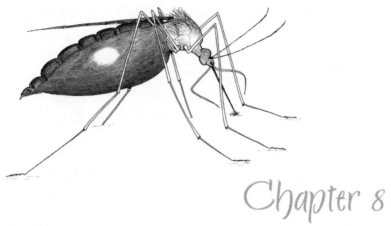

Chapter 8

Buffalo Herds, Beer and a Disease-Free World

A herd of buffalo can only move as fast as the slowest buffalo. And when the herd is hunted by wolves and mountain lions, it is the slowest and weakest ones at the back that are killed first. This natural selection is good for the herd as a whole, because the general speed and health of the whole group keeps improving by the regular killing of the weakest members.

This natural culling process affects all living things. When baby sloths tumble from the tops of tall trees, sometimes they die, but often they suffer little or no damage from the fall. Even though unharmed from the fall these infants are doomed. If they don't fall prey to a predator or scavenger, starvation comes quickly. The interesting thing is that the mother sloth makes no attempt to rescue her baby, even when humans intervene and try to return it to her. The mothering instinct has its limits where species survival is at stake.

Another example is the great barrier reef of Australia, one of the great natural wonders of the world. The outside of the reef takes an incredible beating from great waves which come rolling unimpeded across the Pacific Ocean. On the inside of the great barrier reef the sea is calm and the coral has an easy life. Our first reflection may tell us that inside the reef the coral will be in excellent healthy condition and outside it will be tattered, broken and damaged from the constant battering. In reality, exactly the opposite is true. On the outside the weak and defective coral is eliminated, and that which survives to pass on its genes is the strongest and most vigorous. On the inside of the reef, without the intense natural selection, the coral tends to degenerate.

Think of an elite soldier who, under adverse conditions, pushes his body and mind to the limit every day. Now imagine an overweight office worker whose most strenuous physical exertion is clicking his mouse, lifting his coffee cup and dunking his donut. Which of the two is better equipped to survive hardship?

Humans are not exempt from natural selection. In primitive societies where hospital care is nonexistent, the weaker individuals who are unable to resist disease and the rigors of life simply die. A woman whose pelvis is too narrow for her to give birth will die during labor, and neither she nor her child will pass on the genes for a narrow pelvis. Those who bring no benefit to the population as a whole perish naturally or by cultural convention. When they become a burden to the rest of the tribe, the elderly in some primitive societies will submit themselves to Mother Nature who will mercifully end their life cycle. This is the case with Eskimos where older people who can no longer keep up with the migrating tribe sit on the ice and wait for the polar bear to take them into the next world. In Australia the aborigines always put the oldest passenger in the last seat of the canoe, the position most vulnerable to crocodile attack. In Borneo, some tribes have improved on this theme by putting the mother-in-law in the tail end of the canoe, an excellent example of primitive people's true ingenuity.

As a student, more years ago than I care to remember, I was taught that civilized humans are pretty much apart from nature and are, in fact, far superior to it. With a really big brain and an opposable thumb, our destiny is to dominate nature, control it and bend it to serve our own needs. As proof of our superiority I was taught that, among other triumphs, we had already eradicated smallpox, and were well on the way to doing the same with tuberculosis and malaria. The big news in science was that by the turn of the century, forty years in the future, we would live in a "disease-free" world.

Those forty years have now passed and so has the turn of the century. According to the World Health Organization, well over two million people died of tuberculosis in 1998. AIDS, a disease that didn't even exist when I was in school, kills about a million people each year, and that isn't even enough to get it a place in the top ten fatal diseases. Mad cow disease is another new one. This infection is caused by something called a prion that can't even be destroyed by fire. Smallpox, which we "eradicated" many years ago is now showing signs of revival. Our medicines seem to be more expensive than ever before and less effective.

So what happened to our dominion over nature? What went wrong? A look at the battle between humans and malaria may yield a few clues. Malaria is a disease that can be eliminated by destroying or controlling either of the two lower life forms involved: the carrier, a mosquito, or the perpetrator, a blood parasite, neither of which has a big brain or an opposable thumb. That sounds like a piece of cake. Let's have a look at what happened in the war against malaria.

Prior to 1950 humans living in malaria-infested regions developed a natural immunity. Everyone became infected with the disease at an early age; the weakest and least fit died as infants and the strongest survived. Those who survived were immune for about a year, and reinfection continually renewed their natural defenses against malaria, much like a booster vaccine. The process of natural selection had created an equilibrium or standoff between humans and malaria. The disease was a major cause of infant mortality, but people had learned to live with it.

Then civilized humans put those really big brains to work and invented a chemical called dichloro-diphenyl-trichloroethane, more commonly known as DDT. This was the big gun that was going to finish off malaria once and for all. It was just the weapon needed to eradicate *Anopheline* mosquitoes, the principal carriers of the disease. War was declared against mosquitoes. In the 1950s and 1960s, millions of tons of DDT were sprayed all over the world, on wetlands where mosquitoes breed and in homes where they infect people. No place that might harbor malaria-bearing mosquitoes was spared. Uncounted billions of mosquitoes died. The ultimate goal of the war was the total extinction of *Anopheles* mosquitoes, and it soon became apparent that victory would likely be achieved.

But the war against mosquitoes was only one battlefront. *Anopheles* is merely the carrier or vector. We can also attack the cause of malaria, the *Plasmodium* blood parasite. The first effective treatment was quinine, a natural remedy derived from the bark of a tree. It was discovered by the indigenous peoples of the Amazon. They used it to alleviate the fevers caused by malaria and later gave quinine powder to Jesuit missionaries. From there it spread over the entire globe, and the demand for it nearly drove the cinchona tree, from which it is derived, to extinction. Later several artificial substitutes were discovered of which chloroquine was the most widely used. Mass application of chloroquine allowed some of the malaria warriors to rid human populations of the *Plasmodium* parasite while others were eliminating *Anopheles* mosquitoes.

The results of the war against mosquitoes are now history. *Homo sapiens* won almost every battle, but *Anopheles* won the war. Additionally, massive application of DDT did grave damage to a number of bird species, killed off many beneficial insects, accumulated in the fatty tissues of humans and became concentrated in mother's milk. It also created super mosquitoes. It killed off the weakest ones with the least resistance. If only one out of a million mosquitoes survived; that one was the most resistant to DDT and lived to mate with other survivors. Each generation of *Anopheles* was genetically stronger than the previous. After about five years of the spraying of DDT, mosquitoes achieved close to 100 percent immunity. Later they developed resistance to other pesticides as well.

On the other battle front—the war against *Plasmodium*—medical teams distributed large quantities of chloroquine, not only for treatment of malaria but also for prevention. It became the recommended malaria pill for travelers. Several other drugs were developed, but they were all quite similar to chloroquine in chemical structure and really offered nothing new. When the parasite built up resistance to chloroquine it also became partially resistant to the others. Every weapon modern medicine has been able to throw at *Plasmodium* has soon lost its effectiveness. In much of the world the parasite is now totally resistant to treatment by any available drug or cocktail of drugs.

Meanwhile the temporary respite from malaria due to early victories had caused the inhabitants of formerly infested areas to lose their immunity. Once *Anopheles* became resistant and returned to those areas, carrying *Plasmodium* parasites, the results were devastating. Not only that, but widespread use of DDT had been very detrimental to the environment and the people. Some of those problems wouldn't be recognized until much later. In 1972 DDT was banned from use in the United States.

Fortunately, Costa Rica has been pretty much malaria-free for the last thirty years. The war against malaria here has been successful up until now. But, all it would take is a few infected *Anopheles* mosquitoes in the cargo hold of a ship from Africa. No place where mosquitoes live is safe from an outbreak. Millions of Americans were thrown into panic in 1999 when a wave of West Nile fever, another mosquito-borne disease, struck New York City, causing a number of deaths in humans, birds and horses. New Yorkers were said to have developed mosquito phobia during the epidemic.

Let's have a look at the final score in the war against malaria. In the end we accomplished four things: (1) we created super mosquitoes and super malaria parasites, (2) we weakened the natural defenses of humans in malaria-infested regions, (3) we contaminated our own environment with dangerous chemicals, and (4) we produced fortunes for the manufacturers and distributors of DDT and chloroquine. Andrew Spielman, Sc.D., one of the world's foremost authorities on the subject, in his recent book, *Mosquito*, sums up the current situation precisely: "Every year, 10 percent of the world's population suffers from malaria. Every twelve seconds a malaria-infected child dies." That adds up to 2,628,000 children per year.

So much for dreams of a disease-free world. The dismal final outcome of the war against malaria illustrates that much of our modern approach to disease is completely out of touch with Mother Nature. Our attitude of superiority and lack of respect for her has only made us more vulnerable to her whims. More often than not, our meddling and attempts to alter our planet get us into trouble. If we believe the illusion that we can dominate every other species on earth and bypass the natural selection process, we may end up getting ourselves selected right out of existence. Humans continue to combat diseases through the massive use of drugs. In so doing, we become weaker while, at the same time, the agents of disease become stronger and more difficult to combat or contain. We need to find ways to live in harmony with our environment, not dominate or destroy it.

Remember how natural selection works in the herd of buffalo, making the herd stronger and faster by culling the slow and weak? The other day I heard a new twist to it. Here goes: Much the same as the herd of buffalo, the human brain can only operate as fast as the slowest brain cells. Excessive intake of alcohol, as we know, kills brain cells. But naturally, it attacks the slowest and weakest brain cells first. In this way, regular consumption of beer eliminates the weaker brain cells, making the brain a faster and more efficient organ. That's why you always feel smarter after a few beers.

So I guess each of us is going to have to think things over and make a decision. Either we get in touch with nature and go to work for a healthy environment or have another beer and let governments take care of it for us. ᐷ

Chapter 9

The Good Guys and The Bad Guys?

What comes into your mind when you hear or read the word "predator"? An image of the Big Bad Wolf; a snarling bear with bloodshot eyes and white, blood-stained fangs slashing into a helpless fawn; a hawk or falcon swooping down on a poor inoffensive dove or maybe a cloaked villain lurking in the shadows waiting for some defenseless victim to pass by? My dictionary defines predatory as: (1) living by preying upon other animals, (2) characterized by plundering or stealing. My thesaurus lists seven synonyms for predatory, all of which imply despicable behavior. In reality, however, it all depends on your point of view. For example, in western culture, according to traditional beliefs, it is bad if a hawk kills a dove, a lion kills an antelope or a wolf kills a fawn, but it is even worse if a fox kills a chicken, a coyote kills a sheep or a cougar kills a calf. What makes it worse is that humans own these animals and therefore have the exclusive right to kill them and eat them. We raise them and buy feed for them and get them fat first and then we kill them and eat them. Of course, in our case it isn't despicable at all. We need to do this to feed ourselves. I hope you're following the logic here, because I'm a little fuzzy on it. Don't get me wrong though. I'm not saying we shouldn't eat meat. What I'm saying is your point of view makes a big difference and that maybe predators have been getting a bum rap.

In recent years we humans have begun to reexamine some of our beliefs about nature and question some of our traditional negative feelings about predatory wildlife. As we learn more about our environment and look at the overall scheme of nature, we have come to appreciate the crucial function carried out by animals that kill other animals. So critical is their role that the presence of a large spectrum of predators is a clear indicator of a healthy ecosystem. This is especially visible in the tropics where the rainforests harbor a vast diversity of species. Let's look at a couple of examples.

Manuel Antonio National Park, with 682 hectares (1,685 acres), is Costa Rica's most visited National Park. According to Mario Boza's 1988 book *Costa Rica National Parks*, there were 184 bird species in the park at that time. Even assuming that a few new species have been registered in the last thirteen years this number is surprisingly low. On Hacienda Barú National Wildlife Refuge, which is only half the size of Manuel Antonio and is situated only 50 kilometers (31 miles) to the south in a similar ecosystem, ornithologists have registered 311 species. Also surprising is that none of the mammals listed in Boza's book could be considered predators. Several omnivores like the white-faced capuchin monkey and the white-nosed coati could be considered opportunistic predators, but no carnivores were listed. In contrast, Hacienda Barú has recorded twelve mammal predators, including five species of cats. At the time I didn't see a connection between the lack of predators and the lack of birds at Manuel Antonio. Then I learned of a similar situation on Barro Colorado Island in Panama.

According to John Terbrough in *Requiem for Nature*, one of the most intensively studied tropical habitats in the world is 1,600-hectare (about 4,000 acres) Barro Colorado Island. Located in Gatun Lake in the central portion of the Panama Canal, Barro Colorado has been isolated from the mainland since the early 1900s when the canal was constructed. Between 1920 and 1970, forty-five species of birds disappeared from the island. More than half of these local extinctions were puzzling for ornithologists. Several researchers began seeking answers and by the early 1980s a great deal of light had been shed on the problem. It was determined that bird disappearances didn't begin until after the disappearance of top predators such as the puma and jaguar. Once these major carnivores were gone, a rapid increase occurred in populations of their prey species, which included coatis and raccoons. Both of these omnivorous species are partially arboreal and often prey on birds' eggs and nestlings. The population of coatis on Barro Colorado Island was found to be about twenty times higher than in the Amazon rainforest. This clearly explains the local extinction of so many bird species.

Another example was brought to light by hunters rather than biologists. The first game preserves that appear in history belonged to feudal landlords who protected large extensions of land as hunting refuges. Many of these were for the protection of game birds such as pheasant and quail, which the owners hunted for sport. Hawks, eagles and other raptors known to prey on the game birds were routinely killed because the landlords assumed that reduced predator populations would translate into increased game populations. Bounties were even paid for the killing of these raptors. Eventually, however, it became clear that just the opposite was true. As predatory bird populations declined so did those of the game birds. When numbers got so low that the hunters lost interest in the game bird preserve, quit hunting and quit killing predatory birds, the raptor populations soon returned to normal levels and game bird populations followed. At first the reasons weren't clear. Why would lower numbers of predators result in lower numbers of their prey? A closer look at the most common prey of these raptors told the story. Most of the hawks and eagles that had been targeted really were only guilty of killing a few of the game birds the hunters wanted to preserve. Their primary prey, however, were small rodents. Without the raptors to keep them under control, rodent populations increased rapidly. These included rats, which kill many more nestlings and eat more birds' eggs than do raptors. The solution is simple. Let the predators do their thing. Their presence signifies a healthy ecosystem.

Any animal must acquire its food as efficiently as possible. It must acquire each calorie of food energy with the expenditure of less than one calorie of bodily energy. If it does not, it will slowly decline in body weight and perish. Therefore a predator must not waste energy in attacking, subduing and killing strong, young, healthy prey, but instead go after the old, weak, sick and injured animals. This culling process keeps the prey species strong, healthy and genetically vigorous. Genes that produce physical defects are rapidly eliminated from the gene pool by the predators.

Large predators such as jaguars, pumas, ocelots and coyotes need lots of space. Estimates vary regarding the home range or territory of the large cats, but it is generally accepted that a male jaguar needs a minimum of 30 square kilometers (11½ square miles) in a tropical rainforest habitat. A female will occupy a smaller range within the male's. Pumas have territorial needs similar to the jaguar, and ocelots need much less area. In order for a population of large predators to remain healthy and free of genetic defects, numbers must be maintained at a viable level. Again, we find disagreement in the scientific world over how many animals constitute a viable population, but we can safely say that it would be at least 500 over the long term. Since the male and female share a territory, we can multiply the minimum number of individual territories, 250, by the minimum size of territory, 30 square kilometers and we come up with 7,500 square kilometers (2,896 square miles). That's about twenty percent of the land area of Costa Rica. In short, to guarantee healthy populations of the large predatory cats that are crucial to the health of the ecosystem we would need a single large national park or protected area that is equal to one-fifth of the land area of the country.

That is not going to happen, but there may be another way: wildlife corridors. If isolated natural forests are connected together by corridors, the result is the ecological equivalent of one large forest.

Jaguars may be found about 90 kilometers (56 miles) to the south of Dominical on the Osa Peninsula in the Corcovado National Park, an area of 470 square kilometers (182 square miles). Nearby Peñas Blancas National Park has about 140 square kilometers (54 square miles) and also has jaguars. The peninsula contains another 800 square kilometers (309 square miles) of potential jaguar habitat, including the Sierpe-Térraba Mangroves. In other words, the entire area could have as much as 1,410 square kilometers (544 square miles) of suitable jaguar habitat. The problem is that these areas are fragmented by farmland and pastures. There are six environmental organizations working as a coalition to create the Corcovado Biological Corridor, which will connect most of these forests together. Nevertheless, the total area is far short of the 7,500 square kilometers we calculated as the minimum amount of habitat needed for the perpetuation of the jaguar.

On the northern edge of the Osa Peninsula lies the Sierpe-Térraba mangrove system followed by the coastal mountain range. This is all potential jaguar territory, but much of it is badly fragmented. ASANA is working to restore connections between forested areas the length of the coastal range. This is an extension of nearly 100 kilometers (62 miles) that stretches north to the Savegre River and the Los Santos Forest Reserve where jaguars are also found. This, in turn, connects to the Tapanti National Park, Chirripo National Park and Amistad International Park. All of these protected areas combined contain more than enough land to support a vigorous population of jaguar, puma and other major predators. ASANA's corridor project, the Path of the Tapir Biological Corridor, provides the vital link between Osa and Los Santos.

The Path of the Tapir is named after Baird's tapir, the largest mammal in Central America. Weighing up to 300 kilograms (661 pounds) and resembling a three-toed pig or cow with an upper lip that looks like a short trunk, the tapir was widely hunted for meat. To my knowledge, the last one in our area was killed by hunters in 1957. Tapirs still roam in the large forested areas at both ends of the Path of the Tapir Biological Corridor, and it is ASANA's hope that they will someday return to the corridor that bears their name.

The Path of the Tapir Biological Corridor project was initiated in the early 1990s and given its name in 1994. Within ten years tangible results could already be seen. During the dry season of 2000 a biologist found puma scat with peccary hair in it at Hacienda Barú National Wildlife Refuge. He said that other evidence, including tracks and near-personal encounters, indicated that there were at least two of the large cats. A neighbor later sighted a young puma, possibly a recently weaned cub. Another biologist was surprised to find himself practically in the middle of about a dozen white-lipped peccary, a species of wild pig that had been hunted to extinction in this area around forty years ago. In 1998 a lone male spider monkey appeared mysteriously on Hacienda Barú. Six months later a female appeared. A year after that four of them were sighted by visitors and their guide. Spider monkeys hadn't been seen here since 1947. The return of all these species clearly indicates that the corridor is functioning and that it can work to give large predators the vital connecting link and freedom of movement they need to maintain viable populations. By creating corridors we are giving a helping hand to the "bad guys," the major predators, and thereby insuring the health of the entire system. Every species has its own niche. In nature there are no good guys and bad guys. They all play their part in the overall scheme of things and work in harmony as an intricately coordinated ecosystem with an infinite number of checks and balances. The only bad guys are those who have figured out how to beat the system.

Under natural conditions predators kill only for food or to protect territory. Well-fed domestic cats and dogs will sometimes kill for fun. There is one predator that will kill anything that bothers it, or gets in its way. This predator will kill any other living thing that competes for the same food. It has even been known to use chemical warfare in an attempt to completely annihilate other species that create problems for it. As a result of this strategy, the predator in question has become so numerous that it has been estimated that it appropriates for its own use between twenty and forty percent of all the solar energy stored in land plants on the face of the earth. This, of course, has been to the detriment of the millions of other species on the planet which, at this time, are going extinct at a rate of over 10,000 per year, according to Paul Hawken, author of *The Ecology of Commerce*. Fortunately the predatory species to which I am referring can, when properly stimulated, use its intelligence in a positive manner and is capable of recognizing and correcting its own errors. That species, of course, is us—*Homo sapiens*. ∾

Chapter 10
Not a Tree to Hug

*T*he excitement welled up in his chest as young Regulo hurried up the steep jungle path. In spite of the heaviness of his pack, he broke into a run at the sight of the men working in the clearing. Small but sturdy for his eight years, Regulo González didn't mind his task. In fact, getting the chance to watch the boatbuilders was the most exciting thing he had ever done.

"Hola, Don Ignacio," he called, arriving at the massive fallen trunk where the men were working. Regulo dropped his pack, which held the workmen's lunches, and hurried over to have a look at what they were doing.

The trunk was really starting to look like a bongo. At Regulo's tender age, time passed slowly; it seemed the men had been working on the tree for a lifetime. In reality it had only been two months ago when Don Ignacio and his two helpers had felled the giant jabillo tree while Regulo watched from a safe distance. The experienced woodsmen knew which way the tree would fall, but felling a jabillo was a dangerous business because of the latex in its bark that can blind a person. The men covered their faces with bandanas to protect them from the white "milk" that splattered with each chop.

After felling the tree they went to work with machetes and axes to remove the branches. Then they stripped the spiny bark from the trunk, bandanas still shielding their faces. It took two days working with oxen, ropes and sturdy poles as levers to get the trunk in the right position, so that they could start work on it. The massive tree finally lay exactly as Don Ignacio wanted, with the part of the trunk that would be the hull on the bottom. The men went to work with their axes until the length of the upper side was completely flat.

The hollowing out of the inside of the hull was done with fire. Regulo was curious and asked Don Ignacio about it. The boatbuilder explained that it was best to use firewood from the nance tree because it burned slow and hot. It was important that the jabillo trunk not be too dry. The green wood kept the fire under control. Each day they spread a sticky mixture on the part they wanted to burn, lit it, and then added the nance wood. It took almost two weeks to burn out as much as they dared without risking damaging the hull.

The next phase of the work required a carpenter's tool called an adz, which looks a little like a short-handled garden hoe, but much heavier, with a curved blade. With this tool they finished hollowing out the bole of the once-proud jabillo. This grueling work had taken another two weeks, but today Regulo noted that Don Ignacio and his men were working on the outside of the hull. When finished the bongo would be just over 15 meters (49 feet) long and the hull about 2½ meters (8 feet) wide on the inside.

The following week Regulo watched in fascination as a dozen men from the village attached ropes to the bongo and, together with oxen, dragged the nearly finished boat down the mountain and out of the jungle. Once they got it to the wide trail they wrestled it onto a low-slung carriage with wheels, and pulled it to the beach with a team of oxen. There Don Ignacio finished the work, shaping and curing the hull and mounting the masts. Over four months after beginning the work, the bongo was finally launched.

Because of its tall, straight bole and ample girth the *jabillo* tree *(Hura crepitans)* was ideal for crafting the long dugout boats called *bongos*. The tough outer shell is resistant to saltwater, making it a good ocean-sailing craft. The first merchant sailing vessels along the southern Pacific coast of Costa Rica were *bongos*, which traveled north from Puerto Cortez trading basic goods. Locally grown products were transported to the market in Puntarenas, returning with much-needed manufactured products.

The name *"jabillo"* is a diminutive of *"haba,"* which is a bean with a pod similar to that of the tree. In colonial days the crown-shaped *jabillo* pods were often tied together with wire, placed on desktops and filled with sand, which was then used to dry the ink on written pages. This usage gave rise to the name "sandbox tree" common on the Caribbean coast of Costa Rica among the English-speaking Jamaican immigrants.

At Hacienda Barú National Wildlife Refuge, sandbox trees are some of the largest and most impressive to be found. Girths in excess of 8½ meters (28 feet) are common in mature trees. The largest tree to exist on Hacienda Barú since I came here in 1972 was a *jabillo* with a circumference of over 12 meters (39 feet). That tree was hollow, with an opening like an arched doorway and enough room inside to park a small car. The empty chamber reeked of bat guano from the hundreds of furry flying mammals that haunted its depths. That monstrous tree toppled in 1988. Today, not a trace of the original trunk remains, having long since been consumed by a multitude of life—insects, mold, fungus, bacteria—and returned to the nutrient cycle of the rainforest, reborn in the form of new vegetation that sprang up in its place.

Latex is held under pressure within the bark of the *jabillo*. When punctured with a sharp instrument the irritating milky liquid will squirt out. One squirt in the eyes of a woodpecker or wood-boring insect will blind the intruder, probably permanently. Boat maker Santos Rios of Uvita, who was almost totally blind by the age of fifty, attributes his blindness partially to having worked with large *jabillo* trunks for much of his adult life. Hacienda Barú guide Ronald Alpízar recalls the day that his father, while chopping down a *jabillo*, was splattered in the eyes with the milk. The elder Alpízar blindly found his way out of the jungle and back to the family home, over one kilometer (almost two-thirds of a mile) from the site of the accident. From the front of the house he called to his wife who, at the time, was nursing Ronald's baby sister. Mrs. Alpízar knew from her childhood that mother's milk was effective in treating the irritation caused by the *jabillo* sap. She repeatedly rinsed her husband's eyes with her breast milk, and within thirty minutes his sight returned. He suffered no after effects.

The blinding properties of the *jabillo* latex were used by some early settlers of this region as a method for catching fish. Although not something I would recommend, people were known to strip the spiny bark from the tree and tether it in a gently flowing current of a stream. Then the "fishermen" would run downstream and snatch the blind fish from the water. As strange as this fishing technique may seem, it was nevertheless effective and commonly used during the first part of the 1900s.

One day a couple of visitors to Hacienda Barú and I were dangling from ropes in the top of a giant *camaron* tree *(Licania operculipetala)*, about as far above the jungle floor as a twelve-story building. The sound of gunshots abruptly interrupted our enjoyment of the fantasy world of the canopy. The sharp cracks seemed to be coming from the hillside behind a massive *jabillo* tree about 100 meters (328 feet) from our position. At first I thought it might be poachers, but that seemed unlikely at midday. A few minutes later we heard another shot. The sound was really more like a firecracker than a gunshot, but the idea that someone had climbed the hills up into the jungle to light firecrackers was even more preposterous than poachers at high noon. By the time we rappelled back to the jungle floor and walked down the hill, we had heard a total of eight shots. I mentioned the incident to some of the guides, but nobody had any ideas. The refuge forest guards went up and checked the area later that afternoon but found nothing. A couple of days later I was returning from the same place around noon. While walking directly underneath a *jabillo* tree I heard another shot directly overhead. This one was followed by a shower of seeds. Guide Juan Ramón Segura, who was with me, knew exactly what had happened. As I mentioned earlier, the *jabillo* seed pod grows in the shape of a crown. In the heat of the sun the pods burst with a loud crack—our gunshot—and fly apart. This is the *jabillo's* strategy for throwing seeds as far from the tree as possible. This extra distance gives the young seedlings a better chance of falling in a stream to be carried away, hopefully to fertile ground, or at least of falling outside of the shade of the parent tree, where more life-giving sunlight is available.

Several days later I had the luck to find an intact ring or crown of *jabillo* seeds that had been knocked out of the tree in one piece. The pod was green and may have been knocked down by a bird or squirrel. Marveling at the interesting shape, I retrieved it from the ground and took it home, where I placed it on my bedside table together with some other interesting seeds I had collected. The beautiful seed crown was the most interesting of all my seed collection and was often displayed to guests along with the story of the mystery gunshots. Then one hot, dry summer night in March, at 1:30 a.m., it exploded. Terrified, I came flying out of bed in the dark, banged my head on the wall and landed barefoot on half a dozen sharp-pointed, sickle-shaped *jabillo* seeds. Lifting both feet at once I landed in a heap on the floor, now with knees and thighs punctured in the same manner. It wasn't until Diane turned on the light that I finally came to my senses and figured out what had happened. After an unpleasant application of tincture of iodine to my wounds, I returned to a dreamland filled with the floating curved shapes of dark brown, sharp-tipped *jabillo* seeds.

Today a number of indigenous groups and arts and crafts groups in rural communities are designing and creating handmade jewelry and other adornments from the cat-claw-shaped *jabillo* seeds and other products of the rainforest. In this manner they utilize the products of the forest but cause it no harm. At the same time these local communities are teaching others about the plight of the vanishing tropical forests and setting a positive example for their salvation. Support these groups by buying their attractive crafts. Ask at your favorite gift shop for handmade products made by local groups.

When you think about the rainforest remember the *jabillo* and how one tree has so influenced the history of a region. Remember its many uses and keep in mind that there are hundreds of others out there that are just as versatile. There aren't many *jabillos* left. We have about thirty at Hacienda Barú National Wildlife Refuge. To me the *jabillo* is a symbol of how the tropical forests have sustained past generations of people and how they hold out promise for the future. I find it fascinating and hope you will too. ◠

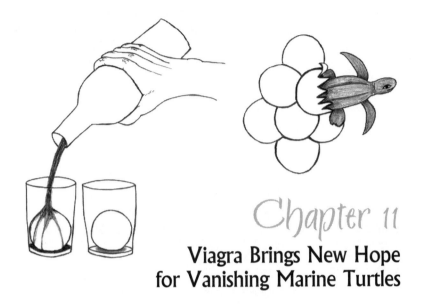

Chapter 11

Viagra Brings New Hope for Vanishing Marine Turtles

*T*he half-moon is waning and has already set, leaving only the meager starlight to illuminate the August night. The ocean is relatively calm, the waves rolling gently out of the blackness with scarcely a brief flash of white from a breaking crest or the phosphorescent sparkle of a simple marine life-form. The tide is rising. A dark shape awkwardly emerges from the water half walking, half dragging itself up onto the sandy shore. For an instant a distant flash of lightning reveals the rounded top of the large stonelike creature steadily moving higher up the slope of the beach. Rain begins to fall; the flashes are brighter and more frequent, the thunder louder. The large animal begins to dig in the sand with its paddle-like hind feet. Finally it can reach no deeper, having dug less than half a meter. From its backside, already positioned over the hole, flexible, leathery spheres shrouded in a thick mucous begin to emerge, each about the size of a golf ball. Quickly they plop into the hole one by one until no more remain inside the reptile, about a hundred in all. Now the beast, visibly tired, begins scooping the sand back into the hole, covering the precious eggs that will assure the future of her species. She positions her hard, flat, bony underplate over the mound of sand and *pushing downward with her flippers, raises her heavy body into the air and quickly lets it fall with a resounding thud, repeating the process until the nest is firmly packed. Near exhaustion, the female Olive Ridley turtle begins her laborious trek back to the water's edge stopping frequently to rest until, at last, the blackness of the sea swallows her bulky form.*

For many thousands of years this scene has been played out with millions of turtles of many different species. Later come the coyotes, raccoons, coatis and peccaries to dig out the nutritious white blobs. Pumas and jaguars kill and eat the defenseless females during egg laying. The ever present ants take their toll. Depending on weather and sunlight the eggs that escape predation hatch between forty-five and sixty days later. With luck a few of the first to drag themselves up onto the beach and zero in on the movement of the waves are able to evade the crabs waiting in ambush and traverse the 50 meters (164 feet) or so to the water, only to confront the many species of marine creatures waiting to gobble them up. But as most of them begin to emerge, a passing hawk, frigatebird or vulture spots one of the hatchlings and swoops down to snatch it up. Other birds follow. Even the white-faced capuchin monkeys take part in the feast. Almost none of the remaining hatchlings survive. Maybe as many as five of the original hundred tiny turtles, less than half the size of a hockey puck, succeed in entering the sea. With luck one female from every ten nests will grow to maturity and return to lay her eggs on the same beach ten to twelve years later.

When humans enter the picture, the marine turtle's outlook for survival deteriorates even further. Dogs and cats, domesticated by people, are the principal animal predators of marine turtles and their eggs. Humans themselves take a higher toll than anything in the animal world. Now maybe one nest in a hundred even survives detection to hatch naturally. Supposedly the most intelligent life form on the planet, man efficiently detects and removes all of the eggs even before any of the other mammals find the nest. Few escape his careful search. The eggs in one nest can be sold to a local cantina for the equivalent of two day's wages. There they are opened and dropped into a shot glass with tomato sauce, lemon juice, Tabasco and *guaro* (a liquor) to quell the nauseating taste and the feel of a raw egg sliding down the throat. It is the "manly" thing to do, and this concoction is believed to make the human male a more potent lover, but the effect, if any, is purely psychosomatic.

The two thin, coarse-haired mounts trudged slowly over the hard-packed sand, their riders slumped in the saddles. The darkness of the moonless night was almost total. The overcast skies obscured the soft glimmer emitted by the myriad of stars. The only sign of natural radiance came in dim flickers of phosphorescence from the salty Pacific foam that welled up with each breaking wave. The rhythmic beat of the surf pervaded the night, lulling the two men into a state of tranquility. Adrian illuminated the beach ahead, the flashlight beam bouncing with each beat of the horse's footsteps. He switched the flashlight off after a few seconds. Batteries were costly. In the brief moment that the artificial light swept over the beach, the men's practiced eyes deftly discerned the telltale sign of tracks on the wet sand. The tide was rising, and turtles that lumbered out of the ocean to deposit their eggs on the beach left a clearly marked path, not unlike that of a caterpillar tread.

The year was 1978, the month August, the moon in the waning quarter, the scene Guapil Beach between the Río Hatillo and the Río Barú. Juan Ramón Segura remembers it well. It was the year he met his future wife, who then lived with her parents near the beach where he and Adrian had come to poach turtle eggs. With frequent stops to dig up eggs, it took the men five hours to cover the 9-kilometer (5½-mile) stretch of beach. By the time they reached the mouth of the Barú River, the soft brightness of the rising moon was just beginning to filter through the clouds. Home was still a long ride ahead. The small horses were now laden heavily with eggs in addition to their riders. Each man tied two sacks together and slung them over the horses' loins in the style of saddle bags, one sack on each side. The night's work was fruitful, yielding slightly over 2,500 eggs, the product of twenty-four female Olive Ridley marine turtles and one Hawksbill turtle. The next day Juan Ramón distributed eggs to all the families where he lived, in Lagunas, sharing with them as they had shared with him.

In the year 2001, twenty-three years later, park guards from the environmental ministry scoured the same expanse of beach nightly for three and a half months, beginning in mid July. They were assisted by volunteers who hailed from local communities like Dominical and Hatillo, other parts of Costa Rica like San Isidro and San José and far away places like London and New York. They spent hundreds of hours walking and searching, always hoping that the next flashlight sweep would illuminate the rounded profile of a turtle in the distance, a rare treat and reward for their effort. The final tally for the season was sixty-five nests totaling 6,822 eggs, all from the Olive Ridley marine turtle, slightly over twice the nightly take of two poachers twenty-three years previous. As in 1998, 1999 and 2000, not a single nest of the Hawksbill marine turtle was found.

The Olive Ridley isn't particularly large as sea turtles go. Weighing in at 40 to 45 kilograms (88 to 99 pounds), it is much smaller than the green turtle at 200 to 230 kilos (441 to 507 pounds) and tiny when compared to the leatherback at 600 kilos (1,323 pounds). Nevertheless, the sight and sound of one dragging herself up on the beach, digging a hole with her back flippers, depositing her eggs, filling in the hole, compacting the sand with dull thuds and then, on the verge of total exhaustion, trudging ponderously back to the sea is one of the most emotionally fulfilling experiences I have ever witnessed. These magnificent reptiles have been here since before the dinosaurs, and I feel privileged to have witnessed their feeble attempt to perpetuate their species in an ever-changing and increasingly threatening environment.

During the year 2001, over eighty dead or dying Olive Ridley turtles washed up on the beaches between Matapalo and Uvita. Biologists don't agree on the cause of death of these turtles, but all the signs indicate intoxication by some unidentified substance. In two cases, vultures that had fed on the turtle carcasses were found dead next to the turtles' remains.

Many concerned people are working long, hard hours to divert marine turtles from their slow steady path to extinction. Since 1987 ASANA, the *Asociación de Amigos de la Naturaleza del Pacífico Central y Sur*, has carried out a project to rescue the turtles. Members of ASANA, volunteers, rural police, and wildlife inspectors patrol the beaches during turtle season in an effort to find the eggs before the poachers do. These volunteer workers remove the eggs and transfer them to a hatchery, sometimes called a nursery, where they are buried and incubated under protected conditions similar to natural incubation on the beach. The eggs hatch between forty-five and sixty days later. Soon thereafter, the newly emerged Olive Ridley turtles are released on the beach and walk a short distance to the spent waves sliding slowly up on the sand. There the silver dollar–size reptiles enter the Pacific Ocean where they will spend the rest of their lives. Between 1997 and 2002 ASANA released over 27,000 Olive Ridley marine turtle hatchlings. Children from fourteen local schools have participated in the releases. A child who once holds a tiny turtle in his or her hand, sets it free on the sand and watches it struggle to reach the water will never swallow a raw turtle egg. Not only that, but that youngster will exert a strong influence on parents and other adults. ASANA has received phone calls from angry parents who say that their children won't allow them to eat turtle eggs. The enraged adults blame ASANA's marine turtle rescue project and environmental education program for this predicament.

Juan Ramon Segura is one former turtle egg poacher who has joined the ranks of those trying to save these magnificent creatures. He is now Vice President of ASANA. Adrian, his companion on that dark night so many years ago, still believes the old wives' tale about turtle eggs enhancing male virility.

The turtle rescue project begins each year in mid-July. ASANA assists with hatchery projects at Matapalo and the Hacienda Barú National Wildlife Refuge. There are organized beach patrols at Barú, Guapil, Hatillo and Matapalo Beaches. Volunteers are welcome. Donations are welcome, and funds donated are used to purchase flashlights, batteries, battery chargers, rubber boots, rain coats and food for volunteers. Sometimes people loan horses so that park rangers and voluntary game wardens may have the advantage of patrolling on horseback. When they locate a turtle nest, they radio to volunteers who go to retrieve the eggs and transfer them to the nearest hatchery. All volunteers are trained by experienced members of ASANA.

Would you like to help? Would you like to come along on a nocturnal beach patrol, participate in a hatchling release? Or would you simply like to contribute to the effort financially? Call the ASANA office at 011 (506) 2787-0254 or visit *www.asanacr.org*.

If any of you ladies would really like to help, you have a unique opportunity to get involved in a way that will make a big difference. It will be fun, too, since it gives you the opportunity to play games with the male ego. Here's what you have to do: When you overhear men talking about eating turtle eggs, simply say "Hey, guys, my man doesn't need to take anything at all to prop up his libido, but if you boys have a problem, why don't you try Viagra? They say it really works." ∾

Chapter 12
Addictive Brown Powder and Biodiversity

According to Aztec legend the tree comes from paradise in the garden of the god Quetzalcoatl. It was brought to earth for the delight of man. Linneas had probably heard of this legend when he gave the plant the Latin genus name *Theobroma* meaning "food of the gods." The Aztecs held the product in great esteem and consumed it in the form of a smooth but bitter hot drink. They pulverized the seeds into a dust which was placed in a receptacle set on the ground. Boiling water was held high above the head in a second ceramic pot and poured onto the dark brown powder. This process was repeated, pouring hot liquid from one pot to the other, until it formed a thick head of foam. Then the beverage was drunk from golden goblets. The Aztecs learned about the seeds, the source of the brown powder, from the Mayas. About the size and shape of an almond, they were considered to be quite valuable and were commonly used as currency by pre-Columbian cultures. Because of the high cost of acquiring the seeds from the Mayas, only the Aztec royalty and the very wealthy could afford to consume the addictive drink.

I'm never quite sure what to call the *Theobroma cacao* tree in English. The correct name in both Spanish and English is the cacao tree, but the bitter dark powder it produces is called *cacao* in Spanish and cocoa in English. Sometimes I just tell people they are chocolate trees, but that isn't right either. No matter what I call it, a certain question invariably comes up. A typical conversation goes something like this:

VISITOR: "I believe I remember reading somewhere..." (studious frown while looking up into the trees) "that in some parts of the world..." (gingerly reaching up and pulling a leaf off the nearest cacao tree) "people chew on the leaves of this tree" (nonchalantly stuffing the leaf in his pocket and grabbing another).

JACK: "Sorry, pal, you're at the wrong altitude in the wrong country, and you're thinking about the source of an addictive white powder, not a brown one. Hey, get that leaf out of your mouth. See that white spot on top of it? That came out of a bird!"

Seriously though, both words, "cocoa" and "cacao," are derived from the language of the Mayas of Central America. They come from a combination of the words *"kaj"* and *"kab,"* which mean bitter and juice, respectively. "Chocolate" comes from the Maya words *"chacau"* and *"kaa,"* meaning a hot drink. These words became *"cacauhaltl"* and *"xocoatl"* in the language of the Aztecs and eventually came to be *"cacao"* and *"chocolate"* in Spanish and "cocoa" and "chocolate" in English. Just remember that "cacao" is the tree and "cocoa" is the product, a seed ground into a dark brown powder that is used to make chocolate.

The cacao plant apparently originated in South America in the Amazon and Orinoco basins. It is not known if the Mayas were the first to cultivate it, but they certainly perfected the process of growing, harvesting, fermenting and drying the beans in much the same manner as it is done today. The Mayas lived in Central America where *Theobroma* thrives. The cocoa drink was quite popular with them and was available to everyone, not for the exclusive delight of the upper classes, as was the case with the Aztecs.

Cocoa was first introduced into Spain by Cortés in 1528. By 1585 the trade in the delicious brown beans had become so important that, by law, it could be exported only to Spain. Two merchant fleets, escorted by war ships from the armada, sailed each year to carry the valuable cargo back to the mother country. The Spanish royalty jealously guarded the secret of the cultivation and processing of the cocoa bean, but the demand grew to such proportions that they planted it in many places including the Caribbean islands of Martinique and Trinidad. Later the British acquired these two islands and the cacao that was planted there. It was the British who took the tree to Africa. The African soils and climate were ideal, and it thrived there. Today the greatest production in the world comes from the small west African country of Ivory Coast.

With the spread of *Theobroma* throughout the tropics other European countries eventually acquired their own sources of the cocoa bean and began producing and experimenting to develop improved methods of manufacturing chocolate. The most important improvement was the addition of milk by Daniel Peter at Vevey, Switzerland in 1876. The only other major advance, which came a little later, was the use of powdered sugar, which allowed the confection of chocolate covering for pastries, ice cream and a multitude of other products. It is worth mentioning that after cocoa is introduced into a country, per capita consumption always increases. A decrease has never been recorded anywhere in the world.

At Hacienda Barú National Wildlife Refuge several different kinds of cacao grow wild within the primary rainforest, and about a dozen wild varieties have been identified by botanists throughout the lowlands of Costa Rica. Nobody knows for sure how these wild species happen to be growing here. The plants may have come from seed stock cultivated by pre-Columbian people or possibly arrived in Central America by purely natural means. I have never found a wild cacao pod with an intact mature fruit. The wildlife eat them as fast as the tree produces them. Fortunately the animals drop enough seeds on the ground that germinate, develop into trees and perpetuate the species.

Between 1979 and 1982 we planted 10 hectares (25 acres) of cacao on Hacienda Barú. Mature pods were harvested and opened by laborers with machetes, the seeds dumped into wooden boxes to ferment and, one week later, put out in the sun to dry. The drying stage was when we all got addicted. The dried seeds look like almonds but have a thin outer shell which can be removed by human fingers. Everyone I have ever known who works with cocoa is constantly peeling the seeds and popping them into their mouths. Even the chickens get hooked and have to be locked up during the drying; otherwise they would eat too much of the production and contaminate the rest with their droppings. But all good things must end. In 1987 the world market for cocoa beans dropped so low that most Costa Rican producers, Hacienda Barú included, quit harvesting and abandoned their plantations. Now we have to buy chocolate to satisfy our cravings.

A variety of wildlife took advantage of the absence of human activity in the plantations and began to come in and eat the cacao fruits. White-faced capuchin monkeys *(Cebus capucinus)* and variegated tree squirrels *(Sciurus variegatoides)* were the most visible. Monkeys feed by ripping cacao pods off the trees, taking a few bites and throwing more than half of the uneaten fruit on the ground. Squirrels leave the pod on the tree, bite a hole in the side and eat as much as they can while most of the seeds break loose from the pod and tumble to the ground. On the forest floor the nutritious cocoa seeds become food for large rodents such as paca *(Agouti paca)* and agouti *(Dasyprocta punctata)* and various species of rats and opossums. The white-nosed coati *(Nasua narica)* does climb trees, but I have only seen it eating cocoa seeds from the ground. Behind all of these seed-eating mammals come an array of predators ranging from the large weasel-like tayra *(Eira barbara)* to the ocelot *(Leopardus pardalis)*.

In addition to cacao seeds the monkeys feed on ants, large insects and many kinds of insect larvae that prosper in the abandoned plantations. Birds like the slaty-tailed trogon *(Trogon massena)* and the orange-chinned parakeet *(Brotogeris jugularis)* hollow out their own nest chambers within the large, black spherical termite nests that appear in the dead branches of unpruned cacao trees. Tamanduas *(Tamandua mexicana)*, more commonly known as anteaters, also frequent these sites, where they prey on the termites that eat the dead wood. Other termite predators include several species of anole lizards, which in turn become prey to hawks and owls. Biologists have been amazed at the amount of biodiversity present in abandoned cacao plantations.

At Hacienda Barú National Wildlife Refuge we have been opening up small areas within the old cacao plantations and planting other native species of trees which will attract different types of insects, birds and mammals and further increase biodiversity. We also intend to harvest a portion of the cacao while still leaving most of the pods for the wildlife. Our share will be made into be a totally natural product.

Organic cocoa is a specialty food that can be processed and marketed locally in our area. Before cocoa reaches you in the form of a Hershey Bar or Mars Bar, it undergoes substantial changes. Some of the natural components are removed and replaced by other substances. The biggest change is the removal of cocoa butter, a valuable ingredient used in the cosmetic industry, which is replaced with vegetable oil. Then sugar, milk and other ingredients are added. The end product is creamier, more heat resistant, sweeter, more attractive, a lot more fattening and a lot cheaper to produce. Everything that is added to cocoa costs less than pure cocoa. With other addictive substances, this dilution process is called cutting.

Chocolate manufacturers would probably object to that term. Locally produced organic cocoa can be processed with the original cocoa butter still in the final product, that is, without cutting the addictive brown powder. Although high in calories, cocoa butter is poorly digested by humans and isn't readily assimilated by the body. That's right! Organic chocolate, locally produced, doesn't make you fat. Listen up, all you chocolate junkies: You can indulge your habit without fear of breaking the bathroom scale.

It has been said that eating chocolate imparts a feeling exactly like falling in love. Maybe that is why so many people love chocolate. ∼

Chapter 13

Blood Eaters Gone Amok

The old man showed me the small wound on the back of his neck. It didn't look too bad. The edges were crusted with dried blood, but it wasn't inflamed. The round cut looked like a small piece of flesh had been scooped out. It would probably leave a tiny scar similar to a pock mark. I dabbed some iodine on it for him. Don Rafael wasn't concerned. "If it weren't for the blood on the sheets," he said, "I probably wouldn't have noticed the cut." The next day he had a second wound less than a centimeter (less than ½ inch) from the first. Like the one from the night before Don Rafael didn't know how he had acquired it. That night another blood encrusted hole appeared about 5 centimeters (2 inches) from the first two. The area around the wounds was showing signs of a low grade infection. In addition to the tincture of iodine from the medicine cabinet, I applied some antibiotic creme to combat the infection. Don Rafael was starting to get worried. He told me that he was afraid to sleep at night. Later that day I took Don Rafael a mosquito net. That night he slept under the net with the edges tucked under his mattress. No new wounds appeared for the next two nights. Then, on the sixth night he failed to tuck the net under the mattress. He awoke the next morning with another wound on his neck and the culprit was trapped inside the mosquito net with him.

The common vampire bat *(Desmodus rotundus)* was dead when Don Rafael showed it to me. It was small, no bigger than a house mouse, and weighed less than an ounce. The hair was reddish-brown. I opened its mouth with a pencil. The incisors were long and sharp. Obviously, this tiny flying mammal was what had been biting the old man while he slept. It had probably landed on his bed, crawled up to his neck and made a small cut with the razor sharp end of an incisor. The level of sharpness was so keen that Don Rafael didn't feel it and didn't wake up. As blood oozed from the wound the vampire bat lapped it up with its long tongue. The anticoagulant in its saliva made the blood flow freely. Once the bat was satiated, it flew away and left Don Rafael sleeping, his blood dripping onto the sheets.

I took Don Rafael to the local health center in Hatillo. Rolando, the paramedic, wasn't alarmed by the bites. The infection was under control. I asked about rabies, but Rolando just shrugged and said that wasn't a concern. In the last couple of weeks there had been one other case of vampire bat wound reported. Rolando said he would report both cases to the Health Ministry in Quepos. Later, I learned that there had been several cases in Dominicalito as well.

A couple of weeks after Don Rafael's experience, a veterinarian from the Ministry of Agriculture stopped by Hacienda Barú. She asked if the vampires had been bothering the cattle much. That was in 1983 when we still had cattle at Hacienda Barú. I pointed out a

Common vampire bat *(Desmodus rotundus). Photo by Otto Helversen.*

number of animals with vampire wounds and told her about Don Rafael and the other reports of attacks on humans. Teresa, the veterinarian, explained that under natural conditions common vampire bats aren't very abundant. Their population is limited by their food supply, or lack of it. They have to work hard just to find a meal. When the environment is shared with humans and their domesticated animals, especially cattle and horses, food is abundant. With nearly unlimited supplies of blood, populations of common vampire bats expand. Fortunately, *Desmodus rotundus* have only one offspring per year, so their numbers don't increase rapidly. They are normally quite wary of humans and houses. But when their population density reaches extremely high levels, they do enter homes and prey on the people sleeping there. Teresa told me that vampire bats can carry rabies, but that no cases had been reported recently, and Don Rafael was unlikely to be in any danger. Nevertheless, it was time to get the *Desmodus* population back under control. She said she would return in a few days.

True to her word the young veterinarian returned with an assistant about a week later. Teresa asked us to sort out all the cattle with bat wounds. Late that afternoon we separated about two dozen cows and calves from the rest of the herd and enclosed them in the corral. Most of the bloody bites were on their necks and shoulders, but there were a few in other places, including the ears. Then the young veterinarian and her assistant strung very fine threaded nets, called mist nets, in several locations around the corral. The bats tend to return to the same cattle night after night, she explained. She presumed that they smelled the dried blood that had spilled from previous wounds leaving red strains on the cattle's necks and sides. Shortly after dark the first common vampire bat became entangled in the mist net. With gloved hands, Jorge, the assistant, carefully removed it from the thin threads and held it by the wings. Teresa painted the small furry mammal with a jelly-like substance she called *vampiricida* or vampirecide in English. Then Jorge released it.

Teresa explained that the vampire bat would return to the roost where its companions would groom it, licking off the toxic gel. She estimated that for each bat they painted, between twenty and thirty would die. That night they caught, painted and released nine common vampire bats. Teresa estimated that during the night, about twenty-five bats of several other species became trapped in the mist nets. Only the vampires were painted with the gel. The rest were released unharmed.

Rabies epidemics aren't common in Costa Rica, but when there is one the vampire bats play a major role in spreading the disease. Apparently they are naturally resistant to rabies infections, easily surviving the disease and from then on acting as carriers. Most domestic mammals are vulnerable to rabies, as are humans. When vampire populations are high, the danger of a rabies epidemic is much greater.

This episode of overpopulation of *Desmodus rotundus* reminds me of a similar situation with another blood feeder, the mosquito. Worldwide, mosquitos cause more human deaths (over one million annually) than any other animal, by spreading diseases like malaria, dengue fever, yellow fever and encephalitis. When I arrived at Hacienda Barú in 1972, the coastal plain had already seen a couple of decades of rice farming and cattle ranching. We continued cultivating rice at the hacienda until 1984. I remember the hordes of mosquitos we had to endure at that time. They were so bad that repellent often didn't work. Some nights we had to dress in long-sleeved shirts, long pants and boots in order to endure the onslaught. Soon after we quit farming rice the mosquito population diminished to a tolerable level. At the time I didn't make the connection between rice farming and mosquito populations, but it's really pretty simple. Fish, frogs, birds, lizards and bats all eat mosquitos. Conventional rice farming requires aerial fumigation that kills many of these natural predators. The fast-breeding insects develop a genetic resistance to the agrichemicals much quicker than their enemies, and mosquito populations skyrocket. When we quit farming and stopped the massive use of pesticides, populations of the mosquitos' enemies rebounded. This, of course, was good news for us and bad news for the mosquitos. Nowadays at Hacienda Barú National Wildlife Refuge, mosquitos are a very minor bother. Many visitors comment on the lack of them.

Under natural conditions, neither the mosquito nor the vampire bat is a serious pest. But in the examples above, human beings had supplemented the relatively sparse natural prey of the vampires with herds of domestic animals, and eliminated the natural enemies of the mosquito with agricultural pesticides. In both cases it was our quest for food to feed ourselves that made it possible for these species to increase in population until they became pests. This is one tiny example of how our agricultural practices and lack of respect for the other living things has come back to haunt us. In the words of Daniel Quinn in *Beyond Civilization*:

> "This is what happens when we clear a piece of land of wildlife and replant it with human crops. This land was sup-porting a biomass comprising hundreds of thousands of species and tens of millions of individuals. Now all the pro-ductivity of that land is being turned into human mass, lit-erally into human flesh. Every day all over the world diversity is disappearing as more and more of our planet´s biomass is being turned into human mass."

How much longer can the earth support our activities? How much longer before the stack of cards comes tumbling down? Since 1983, when that common vampire bat bit Don Rafael and the mos-quitos were driving me insane, the human population of earth has increased by about one-third. That's over a billion more people to feed in less than twenty years. We are supposedly the most intelligent life form on this planet. We can learn from our mistakes, and we urgently need to learn better ways to interact with our environment.

The truth is that many people are learning and taking action. Things are changing in the region where we live. Land is being restored to natural habitat. Manuel Antonio National Park has been expanded to provide it with a corridor to the Savegre River. A group called COBISPA is working on an Interoceanic Biological Corridor between there and the Caribbean coast. A little farther south, the Path of the Tapir Biological Corridor that ASANA is creating connects to the Osa Peninsula Biological Corridor. All of these form part of an international project called the Mesoamerican Biological Corridor. You can picture it as a mega park with all the formally protected areas connect by rainforest corridors.

In recent years we have restored much forest cover to Hacienda Barú National Wildlife Refuge. I haven't heard of any bat bites on humans since Don Rafael fell victim to *Desmodus rotundus*. Mosquitos are now quite tolerable. If you want to live better and in harmony with your environment, work to restore natural habitat. When we restore natural habitat everything gradually comes back into balance. In a healthy ecosystem there are no major pests. Vampire bats, mosquitos and other wildlife that can harm humans are still around, but their populations remain at levels we can live with. Of course the biological corridor projects mentioned above weren't designed with the objective of getting vampire and mosquito populations under control. That's just one of the hundreds of extra added bonuses that happen when you give Mother Nature a free hand. Try it and see for yourself. ～

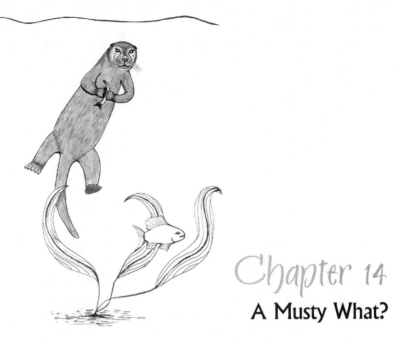

Chapter 14

A Musty What?

No, it's not a musty anything! Mustelid is the word, and I'll bet some of our readers know what it means. Let's find out. We'll start with a little quiz, a quick multiple choice question. Here goes.

What is a Mustelid?
A. A poisonous gas from World War II
B. The cap that screws on top of a mustard jar
C. A rare tropical disease where the eyelids get moldy and smell like old socks
D. A family of mean, stinky killers
E. The self-appointed President of Algunistan
F. All of the above
G. None of the above

Isn't this a great quiz? You don't even have to turn to the last page for the answer. You get it right here. A is definitely wrong. If you're an infant, B is correct; if you're over three years old it's wrong. C and E are remotely possible. Therefore neither F nor G can be correct. This leaves D as the only 100% correct answer.

"Big deal!" you say. *"So what if mustelids are a bunch of stinky killers? What does that tell me?"*

You have a point there. How about this? If you live in Europe, Central Asia or North America you've probably heard of the badger and the weasel. If you're from Africa you've heard of the ratel. If you're from Alaska or Canada you know of the wolverine. And everyone has heard of the mink, skunk and otter.

"Who cares!" you say again. *"We're talking about Costa Rica. We already know about minks and badgers. We want to know about the tropics. What do mustelids have to do with the tropical rainforest?"*

You're right again. What about Costa Rica? More specifically, what about mustelids in the southern Pacific slope, where I live? Out of about seventy species of mustelids worldwide, seven are found in Costa Rica, and we have six of those in our own backyard. This is particularly interesting because, although relatively unknown, as a group there are more mustelids in our area than any other carnivore. Other families of carnivores found in our region include one canid (dog family), five procnids (raccoon family) and five felids (cat family). If the jaguar someday migrates back to our region via the Path of the Tapir Biological Corridor, the cats will then be equal to the mustelids in number of species.

"Yeah, yeah, yeah," you say, *"you still haven't told us about mustelids."* All right, here goes. We have six mustelids in our area: the long-tailed weasel *(Mustela frenata)*, tayra *(Eira barbara)*, grisón *(Galictis vittata)*, striped hog-nosed skunk *(Conepatus semistriatus)*, hooded skunk *(Mephitis macoura)* and river otter *(Lontra longicaudis)*.

"You've got to be kidding. What kind of family is that? What do weasels, skunks and otters have in common, and what on earth are a grisón and a tayra? And another thing, you said that mustelids are killers. I know that skunks smell pretty bad, but I've never heard of one stinking anything to death."

Okay, you have a point, but slow down. Let me take your questions one at a time.

First let's see what this oddly diverse group of mammals, called mustelids, have in common. For starters they all have five toes on each of their four feet. They all have well-developed anal scent glands, which, as you mentioned, has been carried to extremes in the skunks. They have very keen senses of hearing and smell, but they got short-changed in the visual department. They sleep and raise their young in burrows or hollow logs. Although classified as carnivores, most tropical mustelids also eat fruit, the otter being the sole exception.

Mustelids are generally known for their ferocity. Some of them are capable of killing prey much larger than themselves. They typically kill with a powerful bite to the back of the neck. Here skunks seem to be the exception, but even they regularly kill small vertebrates and birds. The otter is invincible in the water and is a very agile killer, but doesn't reek like the others, presumably because of its watery habitat. The most typical mustelids are the weasel, tayra and *grisón*, all of which are adept stalkers and hunters that fully live up to the stereotype of the stinky killer. You probably already know about weasels, but lets have a closer look at the other two.

In more than thirty years of living in this region I have seen only nine *grisóns*, four pairs and one single. I know many local people who have never seen one and don't know what they are. Those who have seen them usually don't know what they are called. Those who do, call them *musas*. The *grisón* is considered rare and very little is known about them. Their scarcity has earned them a place in the CITES Appendix III, which protects them internationally, and they are also afforded protection under the Costa Rican endangered species law.

The *grisón's* appearance reminds me of a badger, only much longer and sleeker. Its body is mostly black to dark gray with a white stripe across the forehead and back to the shoulder. An adult weighs about 3 kilograms (6½ pounds), is half a meter (20 inches) long and approximately 20 centimeters (8 inches) high at the shoulder.

Notwithstanding its small size, the *grisón's* manner reeks of arrogance, not unlike that of a bully who knows that nobody will mess with him.

When we first built the cabins at Hacienda Barú, we made it a practice never to mow the patch of lawn between the cabins and the restaurant. The weeds prospered there, attracting many small seed-eating birds, to the delight of our visitors. One morning a guest arose at 6:00 a.m. to go birding. When he walked out the door of his cabin he encountered a *grisón* sitting in the middle of the driveway eating a rat. Oblivious of the surprised man the mustelid devoured the rat with great relish and sauntered off into the weed patch. The next morning the *grisón* repeated the performance at the same time and place. By the third morning most of the guests were sitting patiently on their front porches at 6:00 a.m. for show time. They weren't disappointed. The short-legged, slinky killer came ambling out of the undergrowth, on schedule, carrying breakfast by the back of the neck. This is the only solitary *grisón* I've seen. It kept up this ritual every morning for ten days and then disappeared. Presumably it finished off all the rats in our weed garden and moved on to better hunting grounds.

I once saw a pair of *grisóns* run across the road. I was a little surprised at their haste, because they normally strut around as if they own the whole world. Upon approaching I saw the reason for the hurry. The pair were pursuing a large green iguana *(Iguana iguana)* half-again as long as either *grisón* and a little heavier. As I approached to within 10 meters (33 feet), one *grisón* hid in the underbrush, but the other had caught the iguana by a back foot and wasn't about to release its bite just because some human was approaching in a car. The iguana reacted to the situation by playing dead. This ploy will usually fool a dog, who will drop the catatonic reptile and lay down beside it to pant, basking proudly in the afterglow of success. The moment the dog glances the other way, the iguana is off and up a tree. The *grisón*, however, was much too smart to fall for this ruse.

It pulled back on the iguana's foot with a quick jerk, released its bite and immediately lunged forward clamping its sharp teeth into the iguana's thigh. The next bite moved forward to a front leg and the third one went for the kill, deep into the side of the iguana's neck. The whole maneuver took less than ten seconds. The *grisón* dragged the dead reptile back into the underbrush to share with its mate.

The *grisón's* close cousin, the tayra, known locally as the *tolomuco*, is an equally intelligent and agile hunter, with the advantage of being an excellent climber. Unlike the *grisón*, the tayra is very wary of humans and quickly runs for cover upon detecting one. These sleek mustelids, about twice the size of a large house cat, are often seen running across the road, but usually all you get to see is a black streak. A farmyard is another good place to catch a glimpse of one. The *tolomuco* has a bad reputation as a chicken killer, and will often approach houses where wandering fowl may be found.

I once had the good fortune to observe three tayras playing in the top of a tall tree. The base of the tree was rooted well down the hill from my ridgetop position, putting the crown at about my eye-level and around 20 meters (66 feet) away. For fifteen minutes the three mustelids were unaware of my presence. Eventually the breeze changed and the tayras caught my scent. Their demeanor changed abruptly from playfulness to full alert. Frantically they searched for the source of human scent. One walked cautiously out on a long branch directly toward my position finally spotting me with only ten meters (33 feet) of thin air separating us. The tayra bared its teeth and snarled audibly, an unmistakable warning. The others started down the tree. I stared in awe as they went head first down the tall straight bole of the *lechoso* tree *(Brosimum utile)*. Once they reached the ground the tayras quickly disappeared into the jungle.

Pedro Porras, a veteran guide at Hacienda Barú National Wildlife Refuge, once came across three tayras attacking a two-toed sloth *(Choloepus hoffmanni)*.

"The sloth was torn up pretty badly and bleeding," relates Pedro. "The three *tolomucos* were trying to reach him, but he had escaped out onto a long hanging vine where they couldn't get to him."

Since the tayras climb with catlike claws, they were unable to follow the sloth out onto the vine where it could easily cling with powerful, grasping nails. These tayras were so intent on reaching the sloth that they were oblivious to the group of visitors and their guide. The human observers stood watching and photographing the spectacle for about twenty minutes. Pedro described the sloth's wounds as extensive and speculated that it probably eventually died from them.

Pedro seems to have an affinity for *tolomucos*. On another occasion he called one up to within 4 meters (13 feet) of a group of visitors. He says he's not sure how, but that he just tried to imitate the huffing, hissing sound they sometimes make, and the tayra walked right toward the motionless humans, stared at them for a few moments and then fled.

The presence of six mustelids and eleven other carnivores in this region is a clear sign of a healthy ecosystem. Meat eaters are the top of the food chain, and only a well-balanced environment will support a large enough prey base to keep their populations stable. If the carnivore's needs occasionally clash with those of humans, we should learn to be tolerant. If a *tolomuco* kills your chickens, maybe you should build a pen. We humans are arguably the most intelligent animal on earth and are quite capable of inventing ways to protect our domestic animals without destroying the wildlife. Mustelids probably kill many more rats than they do barnyard fowl. A chicken now and then is a small price to pay for the rodent control service provided by the *tolomucos* and *grisóns*. Remember, the mustelids were here first. We are the invaders and should always respect our natural environment and look for ways to live in harmony with it. ᶜᵂ

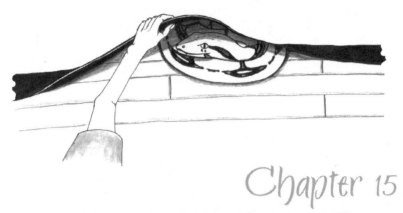

Chapter 15

Bats in the Attic...Pigs on the Plane... Hey Ma, the Well's Gone Dry

My favorite definition of a crazy person is someone who has a persistent problem and repeatedly applies the same solution, with the same disastrous results, while fully expecting a different outcome each time. Politicians are especially good at this. Giving up on an unworkable solution would be an admission of failure. Politicians never admit anything. I like solutions that work. I'm continually amazed at some of the ridiculous solutions we apply to our biggest problems, each time with the same dismal result. Let's look at a few solutions that work, or would work, if given a chance.

We used to have a lot of bats in our attic. The fine dried guano would slowly filter down through the ceiling and cover everything in our living quarters. An attempt to seal the attic didn't work. The bats always found a way in. Masking off the cracks in the ceiling with tape slowed the filtration of bat guano dust, but not enough. Next I climbed up into the hot, dark, smelly loft, crawled around on my hands and knees and tacked sheets of plastic on the attic floor—the ceiling of our living quarters—thinking that the guano would fall on top of the plastic and not through the cracks. That only made matters worse. The bats crawled under the plastic to sleep, probably because it was darker there. Finally, I decided that we would just have to learn to live with a covering of bat poop dust in our house, the only consolation being that guano is excellent fertilizer for the garden. Also, we rationalized that the bats kept the mosquitoes under control. Every couple of months I climbed up into the attic with my whisk broom, dust pan and plastic bag to collect the nitrogen-rich fertilizer, until one day when there was hardly any guano to be found. Looking around, I realized that there weren't any bats, either. "How ironic," I thought. "Now the situation is reversed. The shortage of guano has become a problem." While pondering the situation, I brushed aside one of the old and torn sheets of plastic. It took a second for the brown and cream colored diamond pattern to register on my mind. I gasped a quick breath and stared down at the coiled form of a large boa constrictor, less than a hand's width from my knee. Neither of us moved. A few seconds later, when my heart resumed beating, I replaced the plastic cover and moved gingerly away. The bat problem was solved without my help and with the added benefit that we could eliminate rat poison from our shopping list as well. A family meeting resulted in a decision to live with the snake and without bats, rats or guano.

Now let's have a look at a different kind of problem. Since the terrorist attacks of September 11, 2001, fear of flying is having a noticeable effect on tourism in Costa Rica. One solution that has been suggested is putting a pig on every airplane to enhance airline security, since Muslims would be horrified by the thought of being buried with a pig. That might help with the security problem, but there are probably a lot of passengers who wouldn't enjoy flying with a stinking pig.

Incidents like that guy who walked through the security system at O'Hare with nine knives, a can of mace and a stun gun in his carry-on shake people's confidence and discourage them from flying. This directly affects Costa Rica, which depends on tourism for a large portion of its foreign exchange. So what's the answer? How do we give people the peace of mind they need without putting them through a security procedure that will be displeasing at best and petrifying at worst? The procedure must be absolutely effective as well as quick and inoffensive. Making it pleasant would be even better.

Everyone knows that nothing short of a strip search will detect a wooden knife or a bomb taped to a passenger's body underneath his or her clothing. So let's have a look at the idea of strip searches. Forcing the passengers to undress in front of a strange security officer is so extreme that all but the most blatant exhibitionist would find it humiliating. But, being nude is not necessarily an unpleasant experience. As a matter of fact, the idea of being nude is often associated with extreme pleasure. People even go to business establishments and pay to see nude people on and off stage. Nudist camps are more common than most people realize. So why not take strip searches one step further. Require all passengers to fly naked.

Before you laugh, think about it. The entire procedure could be done quickly. At the boarding ramp everyone could enter a dressing room, undress, put their clothes in a bag and check the bag with an attendant. The clothes would all be returned at the end of the flight when passengers would pass through another dressing room located just off the ramp. If everyone were nude there would be no worries about someone carrying a hidden weapon on board and the flight could be very enjoyable.

In all fairness, the flight attendants would have to be nude as well. The pilots could be fully dressed, but their cabin would be sealed off, not to keep terrorists out of the cockpit, but to keep the pilots in there and flying the plane. There would be no hidden cameras showing the pilots what is going on in the passengers' cabin. We want their attention on the instrument panel where it belongs.

Business would be stimulated. New opportunities would pop up. Body painting, which to date has been nothing more than a fad, would become a major industry. Think of the possibilities for hairdressers. Americans are notoriously overfed and overweight.

Mandatory nude travel would be just the stimulus many frequent fliers would need to go on a diet and exercise program and stick to it. Americans would become healthier. A whole new scope of themes would open for fiction and drama writers. Imagine all the new films that would be produced. Maybe Americans would even get over their inhibitions and quit being so uptight about nudity.

Everyone would start flying again. I bet people would fly even if they didn't have anywhere to go. More people would fly to Costa Rica. The hotels, restaurants, beaches and National Parks would fill up with visitors from all over the world. Problem solved.

Let's look at another one. The other night CNN reported that according to a United Nations' study we are in for big trouble this century. World population will reach 9.3 billion in the next fifty years; we need to double our food supply in the same period of time; but we will probably run out of potable water by 2025. During the thirty seconds devoted to the report CNN didn't mention whether or not the UN had a solution for the problem. They had to hurry on to a three minute report about the Dow Jones average having increased for the fourth consecutive day.

This is a very complex problem. If we suddenly come to our senses and get the population under control, quit cutting down our forests, quit devastating our fisheries, quit expanding our cities onto our prime agricultural land, quit pumping our aquifers ever lower, reduce our use of dangerous chemicals and fossil fuels, etc., etc., etc., economic growth would slow down and the Dow Jones average would take a nosedive. That would probably merit a lot more than thirty seconds on CNN.

In reality, this problem is easy to deal with because we don't have to do anything. Mother Earth will take care of everything for us. In the words of Paul Hawken in *The Ecology of Commerce*:

"Underlying all ecological science is the inevitable fact that, given a chance, the earth will eventually restore itself.

The salient question we need to discuss in our communities and businesses is whether humankind will participate in that restoration or be condemned by our ignorance to vanish from the planet."

Don't take that lightly! Mr. Hawken is very serious about it, and, unfortunately, he is right. When Mother Earth finishes straightening out the environmental problems we have created and brings everything back into equilibrium, we may not be around to see the results and, if we are, there won't even be a Dow Jones average.

So what can we do? The best single thing you can do for the planet is to plant trees. Trees remove carbon from the atmosphere and lock it up in wood fiber while at the same time releasing oxygen. This mitigates global warming, which is causing the climate to change in unpredictable ways. Forests hold soil together and absorb and retain water, releasing it slowly. It is better to plant a variety of trees, preferably native species. In the tropics, trees grow rapidly. Unused land quickly reverts to secondary forest.

In the southwestern Costa Rica area there are many nonprofit groups working to restore the environment. Pick one and go to work. Inform yourself about your environment and do something. Look for your own solutions to you own local environmental problems. ∾

Chapter 16

Deforestation, Reforestation and Regeneration

The word deforestation is pretty straightforward, with not much room for misunderstanding. The word "reforestation" refers to a multitude of practices, some that improve the land, some that neither improve nor degrade and some that are downright destructive. The dictionary definition of reforest is: "To replant (an area) with trees." Obviously deforestation must come before reforestation. Deforestation is simple: Remove the trees by whatever means. It implies human intervention rather than removal by natural disaster.

Reforestation brings up a number of possibilities and alternatives. It can mean anything from tree farming with all of its cosmetic perfection of arrow-straight rows of thousands of trees all of the same exotic species (monoculture) to simply allowing the forest to regenerate naturally. There are a number of alternatives that fall between these two extremes. I prefer to think of "reforestation" as something that is done by humans and to use the term "regeneration" for Mother Nature's method of returning forest to denuded lands.

In the southern Pacific coastal region of Costa Rica the first period of deforestation resulting from human activities began with the advent of agriculture by indigenous peoples approximately

2,000 years ago. Little evidence is available to indicate how extensive that deforestation may have been. A rotational type of agriculture was probably used by those early agriculturists. A plot of rainforest was felled and burned, and the land was planted to several subsequent crops, until soil fertility diminished. Then the plot was abandoned and another cleared. After ten years or more the farmer returned to a plot that had been farmed previously and had recovered a certain level of fertility. Though the land was not quite as fertile as primary forest, it was much easier to clear. This method, called "slash and burn" agriculture, is still used today by subsistence farmers in many tropical forest regions.

When the farmer abandons a plot, a secondary forest will regenerate naturally. The tree species in the secondary forest will follow a succession beginning with fast-growing "pioneer" species and, given enough time, evolve into a complex forest very similar to the original pristine or primary forest. Humans haven't been studying the rainforest long enough to know how much time is needed for a stable forest ecosystem like the one originally felled to return. It is certainly longer than 100 years and may take 200 to 300 years.

Shortly after the arrival of the Spaniards in the early 1500s indigenous populations were decimated from disease and war. Several tribal centers remained along the southern Pacific coast, but most of the land regenerated naturally over the next 400 years. When the first pioneers arrived in the early 1900s, they found wild, pristine primary forest, complete with jaguars, tapirs, harpy eagles and scarlet macaws. Their arrival marked the beginning of the second cycle of deforestation.

Armed with iron tools such as machetes, axes and saws, the early settlers were able to deforest a lot of land in a short time. As new technology became available, they exchanged their axes and oxen for chainsaws and bulldozers. Raising cattle was easier than farming but required more land. The insatiable hunger for ranch land went on until the early 1980s, when the deforestation reached its peak. The original forest had been reduced to a mere fragment of its original extension.

Two factors combined to reverse this trend and save the last remaining parcels of primary forest. The first was a government program which provided cash incentives and tax exemption for reforestation projects. The second was the birth of ecological tourism, which replaced cattle ranching as the primary source of income and employment in the region. The former produced tree farms, mostly monocultures of exotic species, and the latter created a great deal of naturally regenerated secondary forest.

My first experience with returning forest to denuded lands began in 1979 when I decided to convert 30 hectares (74 acres) of poor-quality hillside pasture to forest. I had heard of reforestation, but knew nothing about it and looked for advice from knowledgeable sources. One of those sources was the Tropical Science Center in San José. There I was told about allowing the forest to regenerate naturally and how that was more effective in preventing erosion and providing wildlife habitat than replanting with commercially valuable species. I learned how a monoculture, though very efficient in the production of timber, tends to leave the soil bare and vulnerable to erosion. When a single species of tree is planted at high density, little sunlight penetrates to soil level to fuel the understory plants that normally thrive there. These are important because they hold the soil together while providing shelter for wildlife. I made the decision to use the natural method of returning the pasture to forest. The land bordered a large primary forest which served as a vast seed bank, providing genetic material for the natural succession process. All we did was quit chopping the weeds. Mother Nature did the planting. The two aerial photos (see the color inset), one from 1972 and the other from 2002, show the result.

Hacienda Barú, the farm where this was done, is today a National Wildlife Refuge. It is the most important tourist attraction in the Dominical area and during the year 2004 received over 10,000 visitors from all over the world. The secondary forest that grew up where there was poor pasture twenty-five years ago is now traversed by an interpretive nature trail where tourists from faraway places walk and enjoy the natural wonders of the rainforest. Altogether, about 150 hectares (371 acres) of land have been allowed to regenerate into secondary forest at Hacienda Barú. In succeeding natural regeneration projects, we stimulated the process by planting, in a random pattern, a variety of native species of trees, many of which are endangered or locally extinct.

All kinds of wildlife soon moved into the new habitat. To date, biologists have identified 349 species of birds, 69 species of mammals, 94 species of amphibians and reptiles, 38 species of butterflies, 47 species of orchids, and well over 100 species of trees on Hacienda Barú, and the lists are far from complete. The land has become in a relatively short time a veritable paradise for ecologically-minded travelers. This in turn generates employment and cash flow, not only directly for the owners of the land, but also for the surrounding community, which depends on the wildlife refuge as a place where visitors to the region may visit and enjoy tropical nature.

In 1985 I decided to try some conventional monoculture tree farming in addition to the natural regeneration that I had begun six years earlier. This was done, not on a steep hillside, but on flat land that had previously been a rice field. Eight hectares (20 acres) of land was planted with a little over 12,000 closely spaced teak seedlings. The reason for the high density was to force the young trees to compete for light and grow straight. As the trees grew larger, the competition for nutrients became intense, and the stand needed to be thinned so the best trees could utilize all available nutrients. After three years, thirty percent of the trees were culled and the rest pruned. The sacrificed trees had no commercial value and were left on the ground to rot. Yearly pruning continued, and at six years another thinning took place. This time the trunks were used for fence posts. By nine years, the thinned trunks were tall enough and stout enough for use in pole construction. By twelve years, they had grown thick enough and become fibrous enough for use in construction and furniture manufacture. That year we used teak from the plantation to build a restaurant at Hacienda Barú to serve the growing number of ecological tourists that came to visit the reserve. The tables and chairs were fashioned from teak wood as well.

By twelve years the criteria for thinning had changed. The total number of trees in the plantation had dropped from 1,600 per hectare to 400, but those that remained were superior individuals, being the thickest and straightest of the stand. Previous thinnings had removed the scraggly, crooked trees. Future thinnings were done on the basis of crowding rather than quality. Any tree with a crown that didn't extend up and out of the canopy into the direct sunlight was felled. When the plantation was fourteen years old, we bought a portable saw mill. We have never purchased a stick of lumber since. All the wood used on Hacienda Barú National Wildlife Refuge comes from our own plantations.

As more sunlight penetrates the teak crowns and reaches the ground, conditions for planting new seedlings improve. The appearance of grass is the first sign. If grass will grow in a given spot within the teak plantation, so will a young tree. When the plantation reached eighteen years we began planting several native tree species between the teak trees. As the teak is harvested and more sunlight penetrates, these will grow taller and eventually become the dominant vegetation. This mixed native species plantation will more closely resemble a natural forest with its higher diversity and will provide an enhanced environment for wildlife. Had I understood this principal back in 1985 when I planted the teak, an Asian species, I would have planted mixed native species instead. Nevertheless, I believe the teak, which requires no chemicals, is better for the environment than the rice field that preceded it. Additionally it provides for all of our lumber needs and thus alleviates the pressure on natural forests.

Reforestation and regeneration, or shall we simply call it forestation, is happening all over Costa Rica. The government's incentive program for protecting existing forest and creating new forest has been a key factor in sustaining this trend. There are even incentives for people who simply wish to plant a few trees at various locations scattered around their farms. Tropical rainforests produce oxygen, conserve water and provide building materials. They create an environment where a nearly infinite number of life forms may find a niche, all of them interacting in a miraculous and intricate balance. A primary rainforest contains more biomass and more biodiversity than any other habitat on earth. It is a rare jewel among habitats.

If you wish to plant trees, think carefully about the land, in addition to your own needs. Pay special attention to the effects your project will have on the environment. In making your decision numerous technical factors should be taken into account, such as climate, altitude, soil fertility, steepness of slope and vulnerability to erosion. Also, your own needs or motivations to plant trees will play a big part in your decision. Do you want wildlife habitat, fruit or lumber? The most important question to ask is: What will your trees replace? Will there be an improvement, ecologically speaking, over the previous environment, or will biodiversity diminish? The longer Mother Nature has her own way, the more services the resulting environment will provide. These services include: filtration and cycling of fresh water, protection of fresh water springs, removal of carbon dioxide from the atmosphere, production of oxygen, protection and creation of top soil and the creation of a favorable environment for countless living species. The more your project simulates nature, the better it will be. Any forestation project should improve the state of the land and its ability to provide the services listed above. In a nutshell, it should increase biodiversity.

Whatever you do, don't cut down a natural forest so you can use the land to plant trees. This is tantamount to replacing a Van Gogh or a Rembrandt with a cheap print that you can buy for a few dollars at the corner bookstore. As silly as it sounds, there are people who actually do this. They feel entirely justified in doing so, because the lumber in the monoculture they plant is worth more money than the natural forest they destroy. In other words: "If it is profitable, it must be all right." There should be a special word for this destructive practice that is called reforestation in order to mask its true face. Perhaps the term "gree-de-re-forestation" will adequately describe it. Or, maybe we should consider that cutting down a natural forest with all of its life forms and wonders of nature in order to plant an exotic monoculture is really an obscene twist to that old saying: "You can't see the forest for the trees." ❧

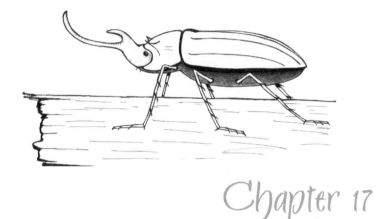

Chapter 17

How Much Is a Tree Worth?

ill's eyebrows went up when he saw the fallen tree. "My god, that thing's big," he said. "That sucker must be worth something."

"We were talking about that the other day," replied naturalist guide Juan Ramón. "I took some rough measurements and figured it all out. If it was all sawed up into lumber there would be about five million colones worth."

"Five million colones? Wow, let's see, at the current exchange rate, that must be more than $10,000. Are you guys gonna use this wood? It would be easy enough to get it out of here. A D-6 would have no problem coming up this valley. You'd have to chainsaw it up into logs and drag them on out, but that's no problem."

Juan Ramón pondered the question thoughtfully as he studied the weathered face and calloused hands of the man who had asked. Bill and Marjorie had been pleasant to guide and had seemed genuinely interested in the flora and fauna on their rainforest tour. But when the fallen trunk of an enormous *iguano* tree (*Dilodendron costarricense*) came into view, thoughts of board feet and dollar signs apparently took possession of Bill's mind. "Come on over here," Juan said, motioning to everyone in the group of five to follow. "Let's see what we can find living on this fallen trunk. It's only been four months since this tree fell, but look what is happening. Lots of living things have already started to work on it. Look at this termite trail. See how it winds along the trunk and under the bark. If we follow it up and around into that crotch we'll find their nest."

Sure enough, the rough-surfaced, rounded black nest was nestled into a crotch of the fallen tree, and termite trails resembling sawdust tunnels were leading to it from several directions. Juan Ramón explained how the termites chewed wood fiber and cemented it together with excrement to construct their trails and sturdy homes.

"If you don't get this tree sawed up into logs and get it out of here," observed Bill, "those damn termites are just gonna eat the whole thing."

Juan Ramón chuckled as he flicked away a few centimeters of the trail with his finger to reveal the tiny termites inside. More of their fellows poured out to help repair the damage. "Do you remember that bird we heard a few minutes ago, the one that went 'yuk, yuk, yuk, wuk?' That was the slaty-tailed trogon. A pair of them always hang around here. They make their nest by burrowing into the bottom of one of these termite colonies. Maybe they'll make their nest here this year, or if they don't, some orange-chinned parakeets probably will."

"Hey, did you see that?" exclaimed Marjorie. "That little lizard...where did he go? He just flicked his tongue out and ate one of those termites, but now I can't find him."

"There he is, right there. His camouflage pattern makes him almost invisible. See him?" Another visitor named Gordon had spotted the anole lizard.

"I see him," said Jill, Gordon's wife. "There, he ate another one. Oh, wow! Look what he's doing now. He's got a big red flap under his throat. Why does he do that, Juan?"

After flipping out his "red flag" the anole lizard took off running up a branch on the dead tree. A movement up ahead of him caught everyone's attention. It was another anole lizard. Marjorie ventured that it must be a female because she seemed to be playing hard-to-get. She leapt from the high side of the branch to the main trunk at least 3 meters (10 feet) below. He started to follow, but then, out of nowhere, came a winged killer who snatched the male lizard with agile talons and ascended to perch on an overhanging branch. There the raptor arrogantly dismembered and ate the unfortunate lizard.

"See what's happening here," said Juan Ramón. "The termites break down the wood fiber; the anole lizard eats the termites and the double-toothed kite eats the lizard. It's the start of a food chain, and that's not to mention the birds that nest in the termite ball, nor the anteater that may come and tear it apart and eat more termites, nor the ants that may invade the colony. This fallen tree is important to lots of other creatures, large and small."

Marjorie found some carpenter bees that had carved a nest into the dead wood and laid their eggs there, and a green and black poison dart frog hopped across the trunk. Then Jill and Gordon's son Jerry called out. "Hey, neat! Juan, what's this thing?" Everyone hurried over for a look.

"I think everyone is missing the point here," exclaimed Bill. "It's fine and dandy that all these bugs and lizards get to eat this tree, but what about people? People have to eat too, and they need money to eat. And this here tree is worth lots of money."

Nobody was listening. Everyone had gathered around where Jerry was poking a stick into some rotten wood at the base of the massive fallen trunk. A huge dark brown beetle as big as a chicken egg was clamoring awkwardly over the uneven surface of rotten wood. A curved horn half as long as its body protruded from its nose.

"Oh, fantastic; this is a male rhinoceros beetle," said Juan, his whole face alight with excitement. "This insect is a truly endangered species. It has a couple of things against it. First, it needs really big logs, like this one, in order to reproduce. Its life cycle requires three or four years to go from the egg stage through the larval stage and emerge as a mature beetle. During that time it needs rotting wood. Here in the rainforest a smaller log would decompose completely in that time and the larvae would never make it to the adult phase. Old growth forest like this where the big logs are allowed to lay on the ground and rot are its only hope. The other thing against it is that there is an international market for rare beetles and this one is not only very rare but also very large and unusual.

"No kidding! Say, how much do these bugs sell for on the open market?" asked Bill. Marjorie fixed her husband with a steely-eyed glare.

Juan Ramón put his foot on a fungi-encrusted piece of broken branch about half the size of Jerry. "Now everybody watch carefully, and keep in mind that four months ago this chunk of wood wasn't here."

With his foot Juan Ramón rolled over the small log. Several small invertebrates scurried away, others, including several spiders, two millipedes, numerous small beetles, a couple of large grubs and untold quantities of ants with their brood, remained visible in the newly uncovered world. Broken ends of a network of thin tan-colored roots protruded from both the trunk and the earth as did small, white strands of fungus. Raking through the aftermath produced a multitude of smaller black beetles, earthworms, and tiny unidentifiable life forms.

"Do you see what I'm getting at?" explained the guide. "All these living things depend on the rotting material from this tree. They eat the wood, breaking it down into the basic building blocks of life, and it becomes incorporated back into the earth in their feces and dead bodies. Nothing is lost. It all gets recycled. When this tree fell, it opened a clearing. With the sunlight that now pours in here, all these young trees you see can grow tall and replace this fallen giant. Look over there, at that young iguano seedling. It's no taller than Gordon, but it will grow quickly with all this good fertilizer and sunlight."

"Okay, so this is just hunky dory for all you tree huggers," started Bill determinedly, "but the facts remain that we have to make money to live and the world needs wood. Surely you eco-warriors think it is better to sell this fallen tree than to cut another one down somewhere else."

"Okay, Bill, that's a fair point, but why did you come to Hacienda Barú National Wildlife Refuge for a tour?"

Marjorie answered. "We met some people in Quepos that told us we should come here, and then we saw your ad in *Quepolandia*."

Juan Ramón continued, "Okay, let's imagine that when this tree fell, we had come in here right away with a bulldozer and dragged the fallen trunk out of this primary forest. In addition to the thousands of species and millions of individual life forms that would have perished, and the healthy trees that would have been knocked over by the bulldozer, and the erosion problems that would have resulted from the invasion of this virgin soil with machinery, just think about how different your experience would have been on this tour today. Would it have been the same?"

"No, but five million colones is $10,000; you could use a bit of that to plant a couple more trees here," grumbled Bill.

"Maybe you should look at it a different way, Bill," Juan said patiently. "Indirectly we are making money from this tree, by leaving it here and teaching guests like yourself about forest ecology. Try to imagine what this forest would look like now without the tree, and ask yourself if the people who told you to come here would have recommended Hacienda Barú had they done their tour under those circumstances. "

"Okay, but you still haven't said anything to convince me that it is better to leave this fallen tree here and cut down another tree somewhere else," insisted Bill.

"I'm glad you brought that up again. Right here we are in virgin forest. Now, for an ecosystem like this to support a maximum diversity of life, you can't take any part of it out. Especially not at the bottom of the food chain, which is where this dead *iguano* tree is. In my opinion it is better to grow wood in plantations and leave pristine habitats like this one to the wildlife. What is important is that habitats like this one have forest corridors between them, so that wildlife can move around."

"That's all very well," interjected Bill, "but not everyone can afford the luxury of leaving land to wildlife. Some people have to make a living, and not everyone can do what you guys do."

"That's true," agreed Juan Ramón, "and we are fortunate here at Hacienda Barú that we can make our living showing people a good time while teaching them about the rainforest. But there are other ways, and people with a little ingenuity are finding them. Some women at the village of Tres Piedras are making a living by crafting and selling jewelry and adornments made from rainforest seeds and other renewable forest products. Some friends up in Dos Bocas have quit hunting pacas (fruit and seed-eating Pekinese-size rodents) and are raising them in captivity and selling the meat. We must look for new and different ways to make a living from the rainforest without destroying or damaging it."

"I don't know," said Bill. "Most of these new ideas never work out. It's better to stick with what's been tried and proven."

"What is tried and proven has brought us global warming and climate change and many other problems. Tried and proven can also mean obsolete. Let me illustrate what I mean with a story," replied Juan Ramón. "A group of scientists put five monkeys in a cage. In the center of the cage was a stepladder with a bunch of bananas hanging over it. Each time a monkey climbed the ladder to grab a banana the scientists showered the other monkeys with a torrent of cold water. After a time, whenever a monkey started to climb the ladder the others promptly dragged him down and beat the daylights out of him.

"After a while, not a monkey in the cage would attempt to climb the ladder, no matter how tempting the bananas. Then the scientists removed one of the monkeys and introduced a new one. The new monkey immediately tried to climb the ladder and was promptly dragged down and beaten by the other monkeys. After several beatings the new arrival desisted from trying to climb the ladder. A second monkey was substituted and the same thing occurred. The first new monkey participated with enthusiasm in beating the novice. A third monkey was substituted and the same thing happened. A fourth and finally the last of the veterans was substituted with the same results.

"What remained were a group of five monkeys which, even though none had ever received a cold water bath, continued to clobber any monkey that attempted to get a banana.

"If it were possible to ask these monkeys why they always punished their companions for trying to climb the ladder, it is almost certain that they would answer: *This is the way we have always done things."*

Everyone smiled except Bill. But the point was clear. We can't continue to do things like we always have. We can't continue to deplete our resources and eliminate all the other life forms that share our environment. We need to look for new ways to make a living without damaging or destroying our planet. ᆺ

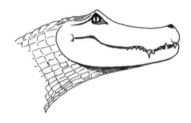
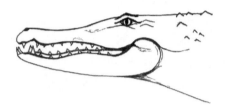

Chapter 18
Please Don't Feed the Crocodiles

My first encounter with a *lagarto*, the local common name for any crocodilian, was on the road to Barú Beach on a hot afternoon during the dry season of 1979. The large reptile looked like a log in the road. I remember thinking it was an odd place to find a *lagarto*. They were supposed to like water, not dusty roads. Then it occurred to me that most of the waterholes had dried up. I started to get out of the jeep to have a closer look, but hesitated to consider the size of the beast. It was about 2 meters (6½ feet) long, possibly 100 kilograms (220 pounds), with a broad head and a wide, rounded nose. It hadn't moved and I wasn't even sure it was alive. Yet its bulk and fearsome appearance kept me apprehensive about stepping down from the jeep. In an instant the *lagarto* whirled, ran straight down the road and then veered off to the side, barreling into the tall grass. Amazed at the incredible burst of speed and power, I remember being thankful I hadn't gotten out of the jeep. I drove to where it had left the road in hopes of catching another glimpse of the large reptile, but only a trail of bent blades of grass told of its passage.

Later I learned that what I had seen was a spectacled caiman (*Caiman crocodilus*). Over the years I have seen many more. Most were smaller than that first one, usually under a meter (39 inches). I also learned that during the dry season caimans are often found in unlikely places. One year a large individual took possession of a portion of one of the Hacienda Barú nature trails and refused to let visitors pass. All the groups had to make a wide detour to avoid the foul-tempered reptile. Another time we found one about 300 meters (984 feet) above the road, up in the jungle nearly a kilometer (almost two-thirds of a mile) from the closest water. I suspect that when their normal waterholes dry up that the best puddles become the exclusive territory of the largest caimans and all others have to go searching for water wherever they can find it. More of them seem to move into the river in time of drought.

One cloudy afternoon in 1989 I was guiding a British couple who were more interested in birds than reptiles. We were peering through a screen of vines and cane that hid us from the nesting area of a large group of cattle egrets and boat-billed herons. The tripod-mounted spotting scope was aimed directly at a nest with two fluffy white egret chicks. I commented to the British couple that the largest caiman in the estuary always takes possession of the water around the nesting area and eats every bird that falls into the water. I will never forget the cynical look that the lady gave me. Her thoughts couldn't have been clearer if she had said, "Look buddy, don't give me that crap. You only see that kind of stuff on National Geographic specials. Not in real life."

What could I say? Maybe she was right. I had never actually seen a caiman eat a bird. I merely assumed that they did. I shrugged and turned to pick up the telescope. To my surprise and delight I found myself looking across the water at a really big caiman eating an egret. White feathers fell from the corners of his mouth as he chewed. I suppose I was smirking as I turned back to the lady and said as casually as I could muster, "As a matter of fact, there he is, right over there." In a few seconds I had the spotting scope on the big caiman's head. Both of them got to see it, white feathers and all.

It was all I could do to contain my excitement. Here was the largest caiman—2½ meters (8 feet) long—I had ever seen chomping away on a cattle egret, and it was just like on the National Geographic specials.

There had always been stories of larger crocodilians. One local cattleman, who tended toward exaggeration, swore that he had seen a 5-meter-long (16½-foot) *lagarto* sunning itself on the mud flats along the shore of the Barú River. Nobody ever paid much attention to him. The late Douglas Robinson Ph.D., renowned herpetologist from the University of Costa Rica, once asked me if we had both caimans and crocodiles. I told him that I didn't know how to tell the difference. He said, "Oh, that's easy. If it's a caiman it will run from you and if it's a crocodile it will eat you." Doug was just joking, but his point was well taken. Crocodiles tend to be larger and more aggressive than caimans, and both are found in this part of Costa Rica. The Tarcoles River has some crocodiles that are up to 6 meters (20 feet) long and weigh at least a ton. I have seen a 4-meter (13-foot) crocodile 23 kilometers (14 miles) northwest of Dominical in the Savegre River near the bridge, in an area where people were swimming.

The first report I ever heard of someone being killed by a crocodile in Costa Rica was in 1994. The incident took place on the Caribbean side of the country in one of the National Parks. The victim was a Swiss volunteer who insisted on swimming in the river at the same place and at the same time of day in spite of warnings by park guards. A very large crocodile was known to hang out in the area. One fateful afternoon the boy never returned from his swim. A year later someone was killed in Guanacaste, and in 1998 there was a death near Puntarenas. In the Puntarenas attack several men were fishing from a boat when one of the fishing lines became snagged on something on the bottom of the river. The fisherman decided to dive down to it to unhook his line. Several crocodiles of 4 to 6 meters (13 to 20 feet) in length were visible on the river bank. The other men

HACIENDA
BARU

photo album

Above: When cacao plantations on Hacienda Barú were left unharvested, the white-faced capuchin monkeys took advantage of this new source of food.

Right: The red passion flower grows wild on a rainforest vine and later develops into a pomegranate.

Above: This young anteater, gobbling down a meal of fat juicy termites, is oblivious to observers.

This *Chilamate* with its enormous buttress roots is the most photographed tree on Hacienda Barú. It is a member of same family as the strangler fig and grows small fruits relished by all kinds of wildlife.

Top: Three-toed sloth with green moss growing on his limbs. *Above:* Female three-toed sloth with 2-week-old infant. *Left:* Three-toed sloth.

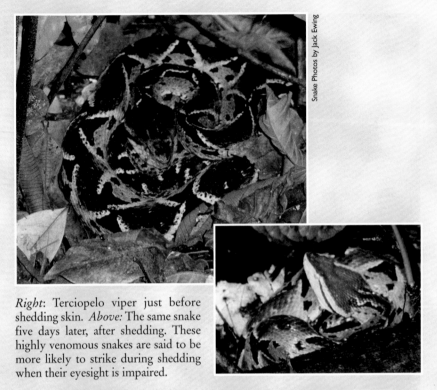

Snake Photos by Jack Ewing

Right: Terciopelo viper just before shedding skin. *Above:* The same snake five days later, after shedding. These highly venomous snakes are said to be more likely to strike during shedding when their eyesight is impaired.

Photo by Deiner Cascante

Bird watching from the base of one of the largest kapok trees on Hacienda Barú, author Jack Ewing hopes for a glimpse of a rainforest creature.

Photo by Jack Ewing

"The Twins"—Jabillo trees that contain a latex that will blind.

Photo by Alan Olander

Photo by Riccardo Oggioni

Red and green poison dart frog, and green and black poison dart frog.

Clockwise from top left: Spectacled owls; birding guide Juan Ramón, focusing on a toucan; the White Ibis uses its long curved bill to probe for food in muddy lake and stream bottoms; the blue-crowned motmot is immune to toxins of poison dart frogs.

Cattle egrets nest in the mangrove at Hacienda Barú. The smaller bird on the left is a fledgling.

Above Left: A common potoo incredibly well-camouflaged in a pochote tree; *Right:* chestnut-mandibled toucan eating fruit. *Below:* Bird watching from a canopy platform 20 meters (65 feet) above the forest floor.

Photo by Jack Ewing

The northern tamandua (anteater) rips open termite nests with powerful claws and fishes out termites with a sticky tongue.

Photo by Riccardo Oggioni

Photo by Jack Ewing

Leaf-cutter ants—nature's first farmers—cut and carry leaf crescents to their nests. Leaves are the prime material on which they cultivate fungus, their primary food *(shown at right).*

Hacienda Barú employees, tourists and young-sters from local schools watch as newly hatched Olive Ridley marine turtles, an endangered species, walk to the sea. More than 50,000 hatchlings have been released since 1998.

Photo by Jack Ewing

Above: Pinto, a three-year-old Baird's tapir.
Right: Closeup of a tapir hoof.
Below: Baird's tapir loves the water.

Photos by Charlie Foerster

The decomposition of fallen tree trunks plays an important role in rain-forest ecology. Hundreds of living organisms participate in reducing a large trunk, like this *Iguano* tree, to its basic elements, which are then recycled back into the environment.

Male green iguana with breeding colors.

A spectacled caiman, 1½ meters (5 feet) long, near one of Hacienda Barú's nature trails.

Photo by Riccardo Oggioni

Newly hatched iguanas are about 20 centimeters (8 inches) long. Their coloring darkens with age. Predators take a heavy toll on the young.

Both Photos by Jack Ewing

At Hacienda Barú National Wildlife Refuge, people of all ages may experience the rainforest canopy. Climbing with special equipment, zipping along on cables, or being hoisted as high as a 12-story building are a few of the options.

Photo Instituto Geografico Nacional de Costa Rica

A 1972 aerial photo of Hacienda Barú as a cattle and rice farm.

Photo by Jack Ewing

Hacienda Barú in 2003 as a national wildlife refuge and eco-tourism resort.

In 1972 Hacienda Barú employed two cowboys and a fence fixer. Twenty-two years later we employ eight naturalist guides, four receptionists, four restaurant personnel, four housekeepers, two gardeners, two carpenters, two park rangers, two security personnel, and five farm workers, in addition to Jack and Diane Ewing. During the year 2004, Hacienda Barú National Wildlife Refuge was visited by 15,380 nature lovers from all over the world.

Photo by Jack Ewing

Self-guided nature walks, as enjoyed by Chris Ewing and his son John, allow visitors to explore at their own pace. The bridge across this swampy area was constructed with wood from teak trees grown in the plantations at Hacienda Barú National Wildlife Refuge. No wood is cut from natural forests.

Right: Owl butterflies.

Photo by Jack Ewing

Photo by Riccardo Oggioni

Photo by Jack Ewing

phone 011 (506) 787-0003

www.haciendabaru.com

HACIENDA
BARU

in the boat begged their companion not to dive into the water, but he chose not to heed their warnings and paid with his life.

Australian aboriginal culture has evolved in an ambient with the ever present danger of large crocodiles. They have learned never go to the river at the same place nor at the same time of day and never to set up a routine or pattern of activity when near crocodile habitat. Crocodiles are capable of leaping out of the water more than half their body length and have been known to snatch people out of canoes. The last person in the canoe is always the victim. This is the reason the Australian aborigines seat the elderly and least productive members of the tribe in the back, and the aborigines from Borneo do them one better by seating the mother-in-law in the tail end of the canoe.

Now that crocodiles have been protected in Australia for over thirty-five years, the species has recovered to the point that there are many large individuals capable of killing a person. At least nine deaths occurred in the 1980s alone. Records show that the smallest crocodile to kill a human in Australia was 3½ meters (11½ feet) long, but most were over 4 meters. To put that into perspective, a Toyota pickup is 4 meters from bumper to bumper.

In 1993 we built a bird blind at the Hacienda Barú National Wildlife Refuge. It is elevated on stilts over the water with netting to obscure the observers from the birds. The large caiman I saw eating the egret became a common sight from the blind, especially during the waterbird nesting season. In addition to the cattle egrets and boat-billed herons, anhingas, olivaceous cormorants, green-backed herons and white ibis come there to nest. One day in 1994 guide Pedro Porras came back from a birding tour to inform me that they had seen a large reptile at the bird blind. "It was something different," said Pedro, "bigger than the caiman."

The new resident turned out to be an American crocodile *(Crocodylus acutus)*. It was around 3 meters (10 feet) in length and had a longer, narrower nose and more pointed snout than the caiman. As a quick means of distinguishing between the two species, we learned to look for the two large teeth, one on each side, jutting up from the forward part of the lower jaw. They are visible when the crocodile's mouth is closed. The big croc has returned to the rookery every year since then during the rainy season when the birds nest. When he arrives the large caiman pulls back into a secondary territory at least 20 meters (66 feet) away. It was two years after Pedro's first sighting before we saw another, smaller American crocodile. Then in the year 2000 a 2½-meter (8-foot) specimen was observed by herpetologist Mason Ryan on a night hike along one of the Hacienda Barú self-guided trails. This was in a swampy area about 2 kilometers (1¼ miles) from the bird blind.

On October 29, 2001, Hacienda Barú guide Juan Ramón Segura, accompanied by tourist Jack Anderson, observed at close range a large American crocodile sunning itself on the Hacienda Barú side of the Barú River on a sandy flat near the river mouth. They estimated it to be a little over 3 meters (10 feet) in length. This is large enough to be a menace to swimmers. In reality there is enough human-induced contamination of the Barú that I wouldn't want to swim there anyway. I doubt if the crocodile would be a threat to surfers. American crocodiles do swim out into the ocean, but probably they only do it when migrating from one river to another. It is doubtful if they feed in the ocean, and I have never heard of an attack taking place there. Surfers, please don't take my word for this; be aware that there is a possibility of danger from this and other large crocodilians.

The spectacled caiman is listed as threatened and appears in CITES appendix II. The American crocodile is listed as endangered and appears in CITES appendix I and on the International Union for Conservation of Nature and Natural Resources (IUCN) red list of species in danger of extinction. The killing of either is strictly prohibited by Costa Rican law and by international convention. I mention this because there has been talk by sport fishermen from

San Isidro of killing the crocodile. Aside from being illegal, I believe killing it would be a very stupid thing to do. Crocodile watching with spotting scopes from the Dominical side of the river could, with time, develop into a great tourist activity. There is a good chance that there are more than the one seen by Juan Ramón, and there will certainly be more in the future. They should be considered as assets to the community. If you have ever seen all the cars and tour buses that stop at the bridge over the Tarcoles River to observe the crocodiles, you will understand what I mean. ➤

Chapter 19
Great Weather for Bare-Throated Tiger Herons

The patter of raindrops lightly pelting the leaves far above our heads was the first warning of a change in weather. It would take a minute or two for the rain to filter down 50 meters (164 feet) through the layers of canopy to the jungle floor. We covered our binoculars with plastic bags.

"Maybe it'll pass," I offered weakly.

"You think so?" queried John, hopefully.

"No, not really, but let's wait and see. When the rain comes this early in the day, it's not usually a passing shower. If we go back, we'll be soaked by the time we get to the house anyway, so we might just as well wait a while and see."

The first bloated drops burst and spattered on the broad-leafed plants of the understory. The sound above was now a dull drumming. John pulled out a small "Write in the Rain" notebook where he had been noting every bird we sighted. He checked the list.

"We've got twenty-seven so far. The red-capped manakin is a new one for me."

"Not bad. We've only been out a couple of hours. With decent weather, we could easily top fifty for the day. With this we'll be lucky to see any birds at all." We turned our backs to a light gust of wind and hunched over to keep the water out of our eyes.

John and I had been planning this birding hike though the rain-forest of Hacienda Barú for over a month. Neither of us was an expert at identifying birds, but we tried hard. What we lacked in ornithological acumen we made up for with enthusiasm. Our bible was *A Guide to the Birds of Costa Rica* with its drawings and descriptions of all the birds in the country. The most difficult to identify were what John called "LBJs," short for "little brown jobs." These were small, nondescript brown or tan birds that, to the untrained eye, all looked alike. LBJs could be wrens, flycatchers, antbirds, spinetails, elaenias, warblers, vireos or something else. Red-lored parrots and chestnut-mandibled toucans were a piece of cake in comparison.

Back in the 1980s when we started the process of converting Hacienda Barú from a cattle ranch into a nature reserve, one of the first things we did was compile lists of all the different species of birds, mammals, reptiles and plants on the reserve. It soon became obvious that this was a task that would never be completed. There will always be more species to identify. The list grew rapidly at first, but the pace soon slowed. Within a couple of months we had iden-tified over 100 different kinds of birds. More than a year elapsed before we passed the 200 mark. With lots of help from ornithologist Jim Zook, the list has expanded to 349 species of birds, all sighted within the 330 hectares of Hacienda Barú National Wildlife Refuge. To put this in perspective, only about 850 species of birds have been identified during more than 100 years of counting in all of the con-tinental United States and Canada.

As a youngster in Colorado, I wasn't particularly interested in birds. I was one of those guys who might make a smart remark about birdwatchers, who I stereotyped as nerds with binoculars and bird books. But after living in Costa Rica for over twenty years, I caught "birding fever." The next time I returned to my hometown for a visit, my first order of business was to buy a new pair of binoculars. Another purchase was a *Field Guide to the Birds of the Western United States*. The rest of my three-week trip was spent trying to identify all the birds around Greeley, Colorado. The grand total for the trip was twenty-one species. Back in Costa Rica, I put a note on the Hacienda Barú brochure telling about the Colorado birding experience and making the following offer to bird watchers: "If we can't show you twenty-one species of birds on a two-hour hike on Hacienda Barú, we will return your money." I've never had to pay off on that offer.

Birders count species sighted and make lists. There are daily lists—like John and I made, place lists—like Hacienda Barú—and lifetime lists, which have all the species the birder has ever logged. A well-known list sponsored by the Audubon Society is called the Christmas Bird Count (CBC). On a given day, ornithologists and birding enthusiasts go into the field and tally the number of species and the number of individual birds identified in a specified area. As the name implies, this official count happens within a couple of weeks of Christmas. On January 3, 2004, forty-one ornithologists and experienced birders participated in the Path of the Tapir CBC, which took place within a 24-kilometer (15-mile) diameter circle that takes in Dominical, Uvita, Platanillo and Tinamastes, and extends from the seashore to the mountains. Armed with binoculars and bird books, teams of birders, each assigned a specific area, set out before dawn. By the end of the day, this group of happy but exhausted birders had notched up a total of 383 species of birds from fifty-six families and a total of 10,292 individual birds.

Two teams worked on Hacienda Barú National Wildlife Refuge, one in the secondary forests of the coastal lowlands, the beach and the river, and the other in the primary forest of the highlands. The most exciting bird logged was the three-wattled bellbird, which wasn't supposed to be at this altitude. The most beautiful was the blue-headed euphonia, which was seen flitting around and eating mistletoe berries. The common potoo was the best camou-flaged and the king vulture the largest. The boat-billed heron took the prize for the funniest looking bird and the cattle egret the most numerous. The final count for the two Hacienda Barú teams was 181 species. Fortunately the CBC was blessed with sunshine, unlike that fateful day twelve years earlier when John and I found our-selves trudging through the mud, soaked to the bone in a tropical downpour, but still looking for birds.

"So, what do you think we ought to do?" asked John.

"Why don't we go on ahead to the jungle camp," I suggested. "It's less than an hour from here and it'll take longer than that to go back. We can't get any wetter, and who knows, maybe the rain will stop."

"Yeah, who knows?" he answered.

We set out for the camp. A bare-throated tiger heron, which seemed quite pleased with the rain, was the only bird we logged along the way. We might have walked right on by, but it growled at us. I nearly jumped out of my boots, thinking a big cat was lurking behind a tree, but then John spotted the long-legged, storklike bird standing in the stream, fishing. Before hearing that growl, I thought it was named "tiger heron" because of the stripes.

It was early afternoon by the time we reached the jungle camp. After fixing coffee and scrounging some crackers from the pantry, we sat down to relax. Now that we were under cover, the rain quit pouring, slowed to a light drizzle and quit.

"Hey, what was that?" John jumped up from his stool and grabbed his binoculars. "Look! See it right there in that bush, what is it?"

"John, forget that LBJ. Look at that tall snag over there. Four fiery-billed aracaris just landed. Put them on the list."

"We can see aracaris anytime. Look up above them at the tip of the snag. It's a black-crowned tityra." John was excited. "Now that's something you don't see every day. Hey! There's that LBJ again, right back in the same bush. Get the bird book. Between the two of us we can figure out what it is."

The rain came back with a vengeance, this time with wind. We settled back down to finish our coffee and crackers. Throughout the afternoon rain came and went. Whenever it stopped for a few minutes, the clearing filled with birds. At one time we had nine chestnut-mandibled toucans and thirteen fiery-billed aracaris in the snag, all at the same time. I logged two birds I had never seen before, a hummingbird called the white-necked jacobin and John's LBJ, which turned out to be the riverside wren. John added five to his lifetime list. Daylight was beginning to fade when the rain settled in for good. We slogged home through the torrent, arriving just before total darkness and in the nick of time to stop a search party that my wife Diane had commandeered to rescue us. It was the best day of birding I have ever known.

So what drives birders to traipse all over the countryside, spotting scope and tripod over their shoulders, binoculars slung around their necks, and bird book tucked in a day pack? Why in the world would two grown men, apparently in complete control of their mental faculties, walk for miles in a soaking rain just to get a peek at a new bird? I'm afraid I can't answer that question any more than an alcoholic can tell you why he drinks booze. Over the years my birding fever has settled down to a simmer, but I still get excited whenever a new species is sighted on Hacienda Barú.

Speaking of enthusiasts, two couples, all birders, once visited Hacienda Barú National Wildlife Refuge for several days. From daylight till dusk, they searched every habitat on the reserve: forested hills, wetlands, mangrove estuary, secondary forest, river mouth and brush-covered clearings. They had logged close to 200 birds by noon on their fourth day including almost every species on their wish list and some they hadn't imagined they would see. The sole exception was the crested caracara, which had eluded them from the start. At lunch, someone suggested that they hang up the birding and spend their last afternoon relaxing at the beach. Three of them loved the idea, but one of the men, a truly fanatical birder, became downright annoyed with his companions. He carried on as if they were proposing to commit some sort of sacrilege. *If they were giving it up, he would carry on by himself.*

"It's okay if you don't want to go to the beach," said the other man. "But you don't have to get mad about it."

"Oh, don't pay any attention to him," interjected the fanatical birder's wife, with a wicked little smirk. "He's just afraid he might see a liver-spotted skinny dipper."

With that, the man stomped off. And, wouldn't you know it, the beach crowd logged the crested caracara. ᘓ

Chapter 20
The Tapirs of Sirena

Wet sand marked the area of beach covered by the high tide two hours earlier. The fresh paw prints had been made since then. The prints were well-formed and clear, but Charlie was looking for a perfect imprint so he could make a plaster cast. Jaguar tracks are a rarity, even in Corcovado, and ones this fresh and sharp were exactly what he had been waiting for. His brow furrowed with disappointment as the trail veered to the left toward the high side of the beach and off the damp sand. The impressions were still clearly identifiable as those of a jaguar, but the looser, drier sand wasn't suitable for plaster casts. The distance between prints increased slightly as if the cat had hurried, possibly leaping or skipping for a couple of paces. The trail continued toward the jungle edge to a large driftwood log. Charlie pondered the sandy surface behind the log with its confusing jumble of prints, impressions and scuff marks. A flat impression was obviously compacted by a large body. An image of the magnificent feline materialized in Charlie's mind, crouched behind the log, nervously moving its front paws back and forth and flexing its claws while peering over the smooth wooden surface. What was it watching? Three meters (10 feet) back from the log the sand had been brushed flat by the wagging of the thick *spotted tail, a jaguar's last act preceding attack. Sandy prints on the smooth trunk spoke of anxious front paws poised for a lunge. Then over the log it had gone in leaps and bounds. Thirty meters (98 feet) further down the beach the paw prints met a trail of three-toed tracks coming from the opposite direction. This spoor turned abruptly back on itself for a few paces and then veered sharply up toward the foliage, 20 meters (66 feet) distant. The jaguar tracks followed, but the prey made it to the jungle in time. Once inside the protective cover of the rainforest the tapir could easily outmaneuver the cat. The jaguar prints stopped, then turned back toward the wet sand where they resumed their course along the beach.*

Biologist Charlie Foerster has been studying Baird's tapirs *(Tapirus bairdii)* in the rainforest around Sirena in the Corcovado National Park since 1994. As many as 400 tapirs may inhabit the 420-square-kilometer (162-square-mile) park, the highest density being found near Laguna Corcovado. His 20-square kilometer (nearly 8-square mile) study area contains seventeen radio-collared Baird's tapirs and several uncollared young. The research has unraveled many of the mysteries about these magnificent mammals, sometimes called *"danta, macho de monte"* or *"tzimin."* Tapirs have been eradicated from much of Costa Rica, which is why they are presently protected by law and are included in the CITES international wildlife protection treaty.

I had the good fortune to spend three days with Charlie in his study area in late January of 2003, where I met and photographed these impressive mammals, the largest in Central America. We were accompanied by my daughter, Natalie, and her two children, Shawn, 10 and Shamile, 11. Those days we spent in Sirena will remain amongst my most treasured memories.

Previously, my closest encounter with a tapir in the wild had taken place twelve years earlier, also in the Corcovado National Park, at the San Pedrillo station. A mango tree near our campsite was bearing fruit, and the ripe mangos were constantly plopping on the ground. In the night we were awakened by a large animal passing near our tents. It fled when we illuminated the area with flashlights. A careful search the next morning yielded a muddy collage of the distinct three-toed footprints characteristic of the *danta*. The park ranger explained that every night during mango season the large ungulates visit the tree and consume most of the fallen fruit leaving little for smaller mammals such as the agouti and the paca.

Charlie told me that the tapirs around Sirena, 26 kilometers (16 miles) southeast of San Pedrillo, do not eat mangos. He has even tried peeling the sweet succulent fruit for them, but to no avail. He tried other things including corn, avocados and water apples, but the tapirs still were not interested. Finally he discovered their weakness, bananas, which they eat with great relish. Curiously, none of the other researchers he has met worldwide have ever encountered tapirs that like bananas. The tapir's normal diet consists of foliage which they pull into their mouths with a long, trunklike proboscis.

Bananas are ideal because they are cheap and readily available locally all year around. When Charlie needs to approach the tapirs to observe their state of health, check the radio collars or take photos, the lure of fresh bananas makes a nearly impossible task easy. By homing in on the signal transmitted by the collar he can get within 15 or 20 meters (52 – 66 feet) of his study animals, but that distance in thick foliage will only give him a glimpse. A trail of tossed bananas will entice the tapirs to come closer. One time he made the mistake of leaving a bunch of ripe bananas lying on the kitchen table only to be awakened at 2:00 a.m. by the munching sounds of a 340-kilogram (750-pound) female named *"Mamasota,"* meaning "Big Mama" in English. There was no convincing her to leave until the entire bunch of bananas was gone.

Charlie has noted another peculiarity about the Sirena tapirs. No other researchers have encountered any tendency of tapirs to group themselves into family units, but his tapirs show a definite affinity for kin. They also appear to have true affection and emotional involvement with each other. Big Mama was one of the first tapirs Charlie radio collared. He has known her for ten years. During that time she has given birth to six offspring. Her original mate was a large male called Flash, so named because of a mark shaped like a lightning bolt on his rear end. Three years ago Flash died, probably of old age, and Charlie buried him. For nearly three months Big Mama returned regularly to the grave site. "She would lie there like a grieving widow," recalls Charlie, "with her head laid out flat on the bare dirt covering her deceased mate's body."

Within a month of Flash's demise male tapirs began migrating into the area to court *Mamasota*. Flash's scent had disappeared from the territory he had once dominated and kept marked with feces and urine. Big Mama was definitely not in heat at the time and was, in fact, pregnant with Pinto, her last offspring by Flash. Nevertheless the courting went on for two months. It is not clear whether Big Mama chose the four- to five-year-old male named Thor, or whether he won some sort of a competition amongst the aspirants. What is clear is that the other five males abruptly left the territory, which Thor now keeps well marked with his own scent. Nine days after Pinto's birth, Thor bred *Mamasota*. The mating resulted in pregnancy and the birth of a male offspring thirteen months later. That baby was never named because he disappeared at about two months of age, possibly the victim of a jaguar or puma. Thor again mated with Big Mama, resulting in the birth of another male, this one named Nepal. In January 2003 Thor, Big Mama, four-month-old Nepal and three-year-old Pinto all occupied the same territory exclusively. During our three day visit I met and photographed the latter three. Thor was just across the river, but high water and large nasty-looking crocodiles dampened our ideas of wading over to look for him.

Water and mud is important to tapirs and they are never far from it. Their three-toed hoof is similar to that of the rhinoceros, to which they are related, and works well in mud. The best opportunity for observing tapirs in Sirena is near the river at dusk. They sleep in thick vegetation during the day and go out to forage at night. Near the end of the day when they wake up and move out, tapirs usually head straight for water. Charlie says that tapirs can remain submerged for several minutes. They will sink to the bottom of a clear pool and blow bubbles. On several occasions he has observed them doing this from a vantage point located directly above. He was amazed to see small fish in the pool swim over to the tapir and scour its thick hide for external parasites—such as ticks and lice—that the fish pick off and eat.

Charlie doesn't believe that jaguars and pumas are a serious threat to healthy adult tapirs. Notwithstanding the ungulate's awkward appearance, they can easily maneuver their large pig-shaped bodies through the thick jungle in a zig-zag pattern that the large cats can't follow. Also he showed me tapir skulls with wicked-looking fangs that can do grave damage to an attacker. A caretaker at the Oklahoma City Zoo found out about those fangs when she made the nearly fatal mistake of walking between a baby tapir and its mother. The enraged female bit the zoo attendant's upper arm, severing it completely and then knocked her down and bit her on the shoulder and neck. Charlie knows firsthand about enraged tapirs. After the death of *Mamasota's* first offspring by Thor she became so cantankerous that nobody could get near her, even with a peace offering of bananas. More than once he had to climb a tree to escape her fury and once the large female even attacked and bit the small tree where he was clinging. After Nepal was born, *Mamasota* calmed down and returned to her old amiable personality. Even so, when we photographed her, Charlie was careful to keep the four of us behind a large log, just in case. Photographing three-year-old Pinto presented little danger, and nothing separated us from him but a few leaves and twigs. Seeing these endangered mammals and sharing their story was an experience I will not forget.

My interest in tapirs goes back to 1994 when a group of friends hiked across the Los Santos Reserve, between Santa Maria de Dota and a place called Brujo located at the junction of the Savegre and División rivers. During the hike they spotted a tapir and saw tapir tracks. The hikers were all members of ASANA. Prior to the tapir sightings the organization had begun the project aimed at restoring natural habitat to deforested areas, thus creating a biological corridor between the Los Santos Reserve to the northwest and the Osa Peninsula to the southeast. I live on Hacienda Barú National Wildlife Refuge near Dominical, which is located right in the middle of the corridor. A hundred years ago tapirs abounded in the entire area, but habitat destruction and hunting destroyed them. As I mentioned in a previous chapter, the last one seen on Hacienda Barú was killed by a hunter in 1957. Knowing that tapirs inhabit the forests at both ends of the corridor, we decided to name it the Path of the Tapir Biological Corridor.

An international project, the Mesoamerican Biological Corridor (MBC) proposes to create a natural passage that extends from southern Mexico to southern Panama. The PTBC is the only section of the MBC that is situated on the Pacific side of the continental divide. ASANA is educating landowners and looking for opportunities and incentives that will encourage people to protect wildlife habitat and look for ways to connect patches of forest. If you own property, no matter where, protect the natural vegetation, especially along streams, wetlands and fence lines. If you wish to develop your property don't cut down natural forest to do so. Instead, build in areas that have already been altered and save the natural forests at all costs. Try to restore natural vegetation between isolated patches of forest. If you like seeing wildlife, you will be pleasantly surprised at the difference these corridors will make. For more information call ASANA at 011 (506) 2787-0254 or visit *www.asanacr.org.*

Charlie Foerster is a totally dedicated and highly motivated independent researcher. He is not salaried by any university or other institution. He donates his own time to the Sirena Tapir Project and acquires funding for equipment with donations to the Adopt-A-Tapir program and the sale of T-shirts, plaster casts of footprints and calendars with tapir photos. If you would like to help save the Corcovado tapirs, you may contact Charlie Foerster at *crfoerster@aol.com.* ᐒ

Chapter 21

A Bad Trip into the Magic World
of the Giant Toad

I never truly understood the meaning of the word emaciated until the day I saw a hairless dog eating a rotten mango. I'm not one to take pity on stray dogs. My wife, Diane, does enough of that for both of us, but this dog was different. He was a walking skeleton, less than skin and bones. It was amazing that he was even able to stand, and if that wasn't enough, his right eye was severely damaged and blind. I took him to the house and gave him a raw egg and a little milk. There wasn't enough meat on him anywhere for a shot. I had to inject the vitamin B12 subcutaneously. He lay down in the sun and slept for six hours without moving. We checked on him once in a while to make sure he was still breathing. At dusk I carried him inside where he lifted his head and ate a little more and then slept all night. It was like he knew he'd been saved, had put his trust in me and said, "My life is yours. Do with it as you please."

He went through several names, but "Rambo" was the one that stuck. Our family is big on sarcasm, but in the end he earned the name. A couple of things distinguished him from your everyday run-of-the-mill canine. For one thing he was a purebred Doberman, and judging from the quality of the ear crop and tail dock he must have come from a pretty high-class kennel. How he made it to our doorstep is anybody's guess. For another he had eighteen lives, about as many as two average cats. As well as starvation, he survived a snakebite followed by a quadruple dose of the wrong snakebite medicine, a full-force kick in the head by a cantankerous cow, diving over a cliff head first, being stolen twice, falling out of the rafters of the house while climbing after a cat, getting tangled in the roots of a mangrove tree in a crocodile-infested estuary with a rising tide, hanging himself from a jungle vine; you name it and Rambo had tried it. I wouldn't call him suicidal. It was more like he knew that accidental death wasn't in his cards and he couldn't be killed. The name "Psycho" would have described him more accurately.

One day we were vaccinating calves in the corral when an abrupt shout from one of the cowboys got everyone's attention. *"Ay, dios mio, ya el hijueputa tiene la rabia."* I looked around in time to see him hurriedly scaling the fence. Then I saw Rambo running toward me along the side of the corral, all wild-eyed, snorting and sneezing, foam pouring out of his mouth and flying all over the place with every shake of his head, just like he'd swallowed a double shot of bubble bath. I went up the fence with the rest of the cowboys. "He'll never survive this one," I thought. "He's finally run out of lives."

An unexpected burst of laughter brought my head around with a start. My son Chris was doubled over on the ground, near that rabid black Doberman, laughing so hard he couldn't talk. Finally, he caught his breath. "That idiot hasn't got rabies, Daddy. He just tried to eat a darn toad." And so he had. But that was only the first time.

Giant toads have a number of characteristics in common with Rambo. For starters they have more than one name: giant toad, cane toad, marine toad and the scientific name *Bufo marinus*. They're also slow, stubborn learners, appear to be suicidal and they show up in odd places.

I read that some computer buff programmed a robot toad to do everything real toads do. It only took him forty-three bytes of computer memory to do it. (This story text has 8,700 bytes.) According to the article, under normal circumstances, toads only act on two different stimuli, both of which are shadows. The programming consisted of a couple simple if/then statements: "*If* the shadow is large and slow, *then* run like hell. *If* the shadow is small and fast, *then* eat it." You can try this out yourself. Next time you see a giant toad on your porch, approach so it won't see your shadow. You will be able to get close enough to touch it, but once your shadow moves across the toad, away it goes.

Back in the early 1980s, the Rambo years, we didn't have electricity at Hacienda Barú. We illuminated our home with candles and kerosene-burning Coleman lanterns. With no TV, we usually entertained ourselves in the evenings reading, playing backgammon and watching the toads eat insects in the dim light. It was impossible to keep the toads out of the house, so we didn't bother to try. When there were lots of June bugs, it seemed like lots of toads died. They would squeeze into weird places to kick the bucket and we'd have to wait until the stench got so bad that we could home in on it to find them. Local people say that they pig out on June bugs until they get so bloated that they die.

Once in a while the shadow movement programming doesn't work to the toad's advantage. This usually happens when confronted with a situation that isn't written into the program, like a medium-size shadow moving kind of fast. I once found a toad with a bat wedged into its mouth. Apparently its shadow was small and fast enough that the toad tried to eat it. Since toads don't have teeth, it couldn't tear the bat into pieces small enough to swallow, and the bat was wedged in so tight it couldn't be spat out. I managed to remove the bat and both survived. Toads can really take a beating.

On school nights Diane would always take the kids upstairs to bed at 8:00 p.m. One night when they went traipsing up the stairs I heard a wet "splat" somewhere on the ground floor. "Did you drop something, honey?" I called.

"No. Why?"

"Never mind."

But the next night the same thing happened. This went on for about a week, and I didn't think much about it. Then one night, I happened to walk into the kitchen at the same time Diane and the kids went upstairs. A fast-moving, medium-size shadow came hurtling across my field of vision and went "splat" on the kitchen floor. I'll bet you've figured this one out. The splat laid on the kitchen floor without moving for about five minutes. I was beginning to wonder if this suicidal toad had finally accomplished its death wish, when it lifted its head, pulled its feet underneath itself and hopped away to one of those secret haunts only toads know. The following night we paid close attention to the stairway, and sure enough, shortly after dark, in the flickering light of the lanterns, that toad—I assume it was the same one—went upstairs one step at a time. And at 8:00 p.m., when those large, slow-moving shadows went up, it did what it was programmed to do: run like hell, and what it wasn't programmed to do: go "splat"!

It seems that *Bufo marinus* gravitates toward people and their homes. This is particularly true during the dry season, when they can always count on some source of water, no matter how meager, near human habitations. Drainage water, damp flower pots, livestock water troughs, anything wet will do. They can home in on water like flies on a cow-pie. A well-drilling company with the H2O divining talent of a toad would surely be sitting pretty. Back in those days our dry season water source was a hand-dug well. We drew the water into an elevated tank with a gasoline-driven pump. No matter how tight the cover fit on our well, and even though the top of the casing was a meter (3 feet) above level ground, at least two times each dry season our water would acquire a subtle telltale repugnance. That meant it was time to rappel down into the well and scoop out the dead toad before it decomposed completely in the water. That was my job, not my favorite, but somebody had to do it. Later we would pump the well for several hours, throw in some Clorox®, go to the river to bathe for a few days and bring drinking water in gallon jugs from the neighbors.

Giant toads have few natural enemies, their defense being a toxic substance secreted from glands located on both sides of their necks. The poison is capable of killing large mammals including dogs and humans. Even their eggs and tadpoles are toxic, and one case has been reported of two people dying after eating *Bufo marinus* eggs. Several species of snakes have evolved an immunity to the toxin and can consume toads with no adverse effects. The toxin is also said to produce hallucinations and may have been used in religious ceremonies by indigenous peoples. At one time it became the drug of choice in Australia, a country overrun by cane toads. Knowing that its consumption was impossible to control, the Australian legislature wisely declined to pass a law prohibiting the popular activity of toad licking. I once read a short description by an addict telling of his experience: "Yeah, man…you lick the toad, and then, like…you *are* the toad."

As you might suspect, Rambo became a toad-licking junkie. That day at the corral was his first excursion into the Alice-in-Wonderland world of *Bufo marinus*. After half a dozen bad trips, he finally kicked the habit, but he never got over the obsession. He reminded me of a dry alcoholic struggling for control when tempted by a whiff of his favorite booze. On those peaceful nights of reading by flickering lantern light and playing backgammon, if anyone in the family got bored they could always get a chuckle out of watching Rambo and the toads.

The routine went something like this: Rambo lies with head on front paws, eyebrows raised, forehead furrowed, nostrils flared, staring at toad. Toad twitches. Tremor runs down length of dog's body. Toad takes two short hops toward a small, fast-moving shadow, a long quick flip of a sticky tongue grabs a beetle. An invisible spring releases, hurling Rambo instantly to his feet, at which point he casts a large, slow-moving shadow. Toad runs for a dark corner; Rambo in a frenzy follows toad, his nose within a pencil-width of touching it. Toad stops. Rambo stops, lies down and stares. The trembling slowly subsides.

The relationship was so intimate that Rambo would always leave some of his dog food for the toads. Rather than sharing, it was probably that he just never had time to eat it all; there was too much going on for that. Once when he left his entire bowl full of food, his favorite toad overdosed on dog chow and died. I think our toads got to know Rambo and knew that he wouldn't hurt them. He could lay there for hours almost touching them and they wouldn't pay him any attention, but his shadow would send them scurrying away. Programming is forever if you're a toad.

Rambo is long gone, finally being done in by cardiac arrest, but his friends the toads are still around. In the calm of the evening when I hear the rolling staccato purr of the courting giant toad, I can't help but remember that lovable, psychotic, toad-licking Doberman that became a legend in the Ewing household. ◡

Chapter 22

Moon Lore: Method, Magic or Madness?

F ew aspects of human experience have stimulated the imagination more than earth's satellite, the moon. We find it woven into the very fabric of our culture, appearing in everything from religion to nursery rhymes. Let's look at a few examples. *Religion:* Have you ever wondered what determines on which Sunday Easter will be celebrated, or if it is merely up to the whims calendar makers? Actually it's determined by the moon. Easter is defined as the first Sunday after the first full moon that appears on or after the spring equinox, March 20. *Fairy tales and nursery rhymes:* There are the "Man in the Moon" and "The Cow Jumped Over the Moon." *Popular songs:* We have "Moon River" and "Blue Moon." *Folklore:* The Harvest Moon is the first full moon after the fall equinox, so named because the full moon rises shortly after the sun sets, thus allowing farmers light by which they can continue working and bringing in their crops. *Romance:* The full moon is said to bring out feelings of love and stimulate pent up passions. *Mythology:* Luna, the mythic Roman moon goddess, was known as Selene by the Greeks. *Superstition:* Vampires are said to fear the full moon while witches love it, flying on their broomsticks silhouetted on the face of the full moon. Also the full moon is supposed to drive people crazy as evidenced by the word "lunatic," derived from "lunar."

Our language is full of references to the moon. My dictionary lists fifteen words that begin with moon and thirteen that begin with luna, an alternate word for moon. My thesaurus lists eight synonyms for moon that are nouns and fourteen verbs. With the advent of space flight and lunar landings several new terms such as moon craft, moonscape, moonquake and lunar module were introduced into the English language. Moonshine, or contraband liquor, has been around for a long time. Moonlight is either the light of the moon or the activity of holding two jobs at once, presumably working by the light of the moon on the second one. The antiquated term "mooncalf" refers to a stupid or deformed person whose condition was believed to have resulted from the bad influence of the moon. The word "lunatic" is derived from the same misconception. Curiously, that exhilarating, youthful activity and manifestation of teenage rebellion commonly known as mooning, or flashing a bare bottom at an unsuspecting victim, isn't listed in either my dictionary or thesaurus.

We attribute many powers to the moon, some real and others questionable or even absurd. There is, however, no fine line where science and superstition part company. Science tells us that the moon's gravity brings about the rise and fall of tides, but will admit to little else. Nevertheless, many lesser-educated people live by their practical experience and orient their lives around real or imaginary powers of the moon that would make most scientists scoff. A memorable occasion comes to mind which involved a veterinarian who didn't believe in castrating horses in accordance with the moon and a horse owner who didn't know the difference. The vet proceeded with the operation, against the advice of local *campesinos*, and then struggled hopelessly to staunch the bleeding. The horse nearly died. On another occasion, a botanist told me he wanted to plant living fence posts at a project where he was in charge. When I informed him that it was the wrong phase of the moon to cut the stakes, he smirked and informed me that he believed in science, not superstition. Four months later, after his stakes had all dried up, he was back again asking about the phases of the moon and the best times to cut and plant stakes. (The term "living fences" refers to the fact that, in the most fertile regions of Costa Rica, the fence posts sprout into trees.)

Much of the daily life of Costa Rican *campesinos*, or country people, is oriented around the moon. Part of this is practical knowledge derived from observation and the use of logic. For example, a Costa Rican fisherman doesn't need a tide table to tell him when the tide will be high. He knows that at either the full moon or the new moon the low tide will be between 8:00 a.m. and 9:00 a.m. and the high tide between 2:00 p.m. and 3:00 p.m. Seven days later it will be reversed. Adding forty-five minutes each day will give the time of the high tide for in-between days. In other words if high tide is at 2:30 p.m. today, tomorrow it will be at 3:15 p.m., and the day after at 4:00 p.m. Granted, this method is not exact, but it is close enough for most needs. It works just fine for the local fishermen.

I used to doubt much of the *campesino* wisdom regarding the moon, writing it off as superstition, but my curiosity stimulated me to listen and observe. Experience is the best teacher, and actually seeing the effects of the moon on living things will convince almost anyone. I think the turning point in my thinking was when I learned about cutting bananas and plantains. I had been complaining that sometimes the bananas I cut didn't ripen well and never got soft or sweet. One of my employees explained to me that I needed to pay more attention to the moon and tides. Willing to try anything, I followed his instructions. I cut several bunches of plantains at high tide with a waxing and almost full moon. To my delight they all ripened evenly, softly and sweetly. Still not 100 percent convinced I cut several more bunches one week later with a waning moon at low tide. Some of these didn't ripen at all, and those that did were dry and pithy. I noticed something else. After cutting a bunch of bananas or plantains it is good practice to cut down the stalk or trunk on which it grew, to make room for new shoots. When I did this on a full moon and high tide liquid gushed out of the cut stalk, but when I did it at low tide on the waning moon the stalk was dry. I reasoned that if the moon can pull up the oceans as much as 3 or 4 meters (10 – 13 feet), maybe it can pull the juices of the banana plant up into the stalk and the fruit. I was convinced.

Much of the moon's influence on plants seems to be related to the effect it has on the fluids or sap which the *campesinos* call plants' *sangre*, or blood. For example, if you are cutting something you wish to save for building material, it should be cut when there is little sap in the upper portions of the plant. Cutting trees for lumber is best done with the waning moon when most of the sap will be in the roots. When cutting with the waxing moon more of it will be up in the trunk and will attract wood-boring insects that can damage the lumber. It is also wise to cut stakes for living fence posts when there is little sap. This tends to ensure rooting. The stakes should be stood upright in the shade so that any fluid present will drain out and small roots will begin to form where the ends touch the ground.

Palm leaves for thatched roofs are also affected by sap. You definitely don't want sap in the leaves used to shed the rain. Part of our house has a thatched roof. The first time we thatched it, I was in a hurry and decided to cut the palm leaves even though the moon was in the wrong phase. After three years the roof began to leak and on the fourth year we had to rethatch it. The second time, we were careful to cut the palm leaves during the waning quarter of the moon and only at low tide. That was eight years ago and so far there are no signs of leaks. It seems as if the sap attracts mold and insects that damage the plant fiber.

You should only prune trees during the waning moon when little sap is found in the upper portions of the plants. There will be less "bleeding" and less chance of an infection entering through the cuts left by the pruning. This principle can also be used to destroy unwanted vegetation. For example, to cause as much damage as possible to unwanted brush in a cattle pasture, a rancher would be sure to chop the weeds during the waxing moon when the sap will be up in the plant. That way the brush will "bleed" and be more vulnerable to natural destructive processes. In other words, he does exactly the opposite of what he would do when pruning fruit trees or ornamental plants.

Ranchers also use the moon to guide them in practices involving minor surgery such as castrating calves. Any wound will bleed more during the waxing phase of the moon than with the waning. Branding is something else that should always be done with the waning moon. I haven't even an inkling of a logical explanation for this one, but I know from experience that if you brand a calf with the waning moon, the brand will heal quickly and remain small and neat. If, however, you brand with the waxing moon, the brand will grow much larger and become distorted. Additionally, it will take a long time to heal and often does so with difficulty.

Weather is something that interests everybody, and the moon definitely affects the weather, at least in Costa Rica. There are a few exceptions, but generally it rains more with the full moon and the new moon than on the quarter moons. Many years ago there was an annual event, called *La Fiesta de la Luna Llena*, or the Full Moon Festival. By tradition, it was held on a different beach each year, in the open air, for an entire weekend. There was a live band and everyone camped out, danced and partied to the light of the full moon. The only time it was possible to have this celebration was in the month of February, at the driest time of the year. In January or March, both very dry months, there was always danger of rain with the full moon, and a couple of times we had light rains even in February. Another full-moon-related phenomenon has been attributed to this festival. Rumor has it that every year when the Full Moon Festival took place in February there were an extraordinary number of women admitted to the maternity wards of both the Quepos and San Isidro Hospitals with the full moon of October. Once the festival was discontinued the October maternity cases returned to normal. If true, this goes to prove the age-old belief that the full moon is a great stimulus for romance.

Not everything is enchanted by the luminescence of the full moon. Nocturnal wildlife generally prefer to obscure their movements by coming out only in total darkness. At Hacienda Barú National Wildlife Refuge the guides know that a nighttime hike will be much more fruitful on a very dark night. The best time for viewing nocturnal wildlife is with an overcast night on the waning quarter of the moon. The sky will be black until about midnight when the moon rises and illuminates the landscape. The wildlife will be quite active early in the evening, probably sensing that total darkness won't last long. Poachers use this phenomenon to their advantage. It also works for marine turtles during the egg laying season. The best time to observe turtles is with the waning quarter of the moon. The female has two things in her favor at that time. The tide is rising while the night is dark. She can come out of the water and up onto the beach and drag herself across the sand to a point beyond the high tide line. There she will lay her eggs, and when she is finished the tide will have risen considerably, making her return to the sea a great deal shorter. And all of her onshore activity will take place prior to moon rise, which is around midnight.

There's one last thing I forgot to mention. The full moon brings out hoards of mosquitos and sand flies. Now don't take my word for this; check it out yourself. But a word of caution is in order here. If you find yourself strolling down the beach under a full moon with that man or woman of your dreams, and that great orange globe rising in the sky awakens pangs of romance in your heart, have patience. Your self-discipline will be rewarded if you can control your passion until you can get under a mosquito net. ❧

Chapter 23

The Law of the Jungle: Survive If You Can

The call came about 11:00 p.m. I was surprised to hear the breathless voice of Yemaya, one of several volunteers working on environmental projects at Hacienda Barú National Wildlife Refuge. She had gone along to assist the guide on an overnight rainforest camping tour. "Jack," she exclaimed, "I don't know what to do. I have a baby sloth. I think it fell out of a tree, and it needs help. I brought it down to the office."

On the overnight rainforest tour we call the "Night in the Jungle," the guide always takes the visitors on a nocturnal hike. During the walk they had come across a very young sloth lying on the ground. Probably it had fallen from the canopy. It was small and helpless, and Yemaya thought it needed medical attention. "What can I do?" she asked. "If I don't do something it will die."

Knowing that my answer was not going to please her, I asked Yemaya to take the baby sloth back up into the rainforest and return it to the place where she found it. I tried to explain that nature's ways sometimes seem cruel. Finally, with this entirely unsatisfactory rationale and the promise of a more in-depth explanation later, Yemaya reluctantly walked back up to the jungle and returned the infant sloth to the forest floor.

In another incident an excited visitor who had been hiking on one of Hacienda Barú's self-guided trails came running into the reception office, all out of breath. She excitedly explained to Diane that a hawk was caught on a barbed wire fence and needed help. Diane quickly found a pair of wire cutters and accompanied the concerned lady to the sight of the accident. Between the two of them they managed to subdue the terrified bird, cut the wire and bring the scared and injured creature back to the office. When I arrived a short time later Diane had the raptor's head covered with a cloth in an effort to keep it calm. A short piece of barbed wire was sticking out of its right wing and twisted around the feathers. One of the barbs was deeply imbedded in the skin.

I identified this bird of prey as an immature double-toothed kite *(Harpagus bidentatus)*. The wing wasn't broken, and the damage didn't appear to be extensive. We moved outside, and I went to work with a pair of wire cutters and pliers. It took about five minutes to free the magnificent predator of its impediment. The barb had penetrated only the skin on the wing, and there was no evidence of muscle or bone damage. As I reached for some antiseptic to disinfect the wound, Diane's makeshift hood slipped from the bird's head. With a quick lunge and flexing of the wings it freed itself from Diane's grasp and took to flight. Landing on a branch a couple of meters (over 6 feet) away, the young kite turned and looked back at us as if to say thanks, and then flew away to more familiar surroundings.

So what was the difference between these two cases? Why did I help the raptor and not the baby sloth? I can just see those of you who know Diane and me. You're probably smiling, nodding your heads and thinking, "What a coward. He orders a young innocent volunteer to dump that poor helpless baby sloth out in the jungle, but he's too chicken to tell his wife to do the same with the hawk. He probably didn't even tell Diane about the sloth." But before you pass judgment, why don't we look further into this theme? Maybe there's more here than meets the eye. Let's look at another couple of examples before we delve into an explanation.

A few years ago a neighbor girl showed up at our house with a pelican in her arms. About half of one wing was dangling helplessly, obviously broken. This time, Diane was taking a nap. "Hi Shirley," I said. "What's with the pelican?"

"It has a broken wing," she replied. "I brought it so Doña Diana could fix it."

"Well, Diane isn't here right now," I lied. "Are you sure you want her to fix the bird's wing? It looks beyond help to me."

"Yeah," she insisted, "I'm sure. She can just cut off the part that's hanging down, just like she did with that parakeet that belongs to that gringo from Matapalo."

"I see," I mused. "And where are you going to get the money to buy fish?"

"What are you talking about?" asked Shirley. "I'm not going to buy any fish."

"Well, what's this pelican of yours going to eat after Diane cuts it's wing off? As far as I know the only thing that pelicans eat is fish, and one this size is going to need at least a couple kilos (4½ pounds) a day." From the look on her face I knew Shirley was getting the idea. It was time to go for the kill. "You're going to need a pretty good job so you can earn enough money to feed it. With one amputated wing it won't be able to feed itself." It didn't take any more than that. Shirley promptly accepted my suggestion that she return the disabled pelican to the beach where she found it. I don't think Diane ever found out about this one. Not until she reads this, that is.

On another occasion a kindhearted gentleman showed up with an infant anteater. He explained that a dog had badly injured the baby's mother, and he was sure she would die. Not understanding the difference between a wildlife refuge and a wildlife rescue center, he brought the infant anteater to Hacienda Barú. I took the baby tamandua to Diane. She nurtured it for a couple of days according to instructions from the veterinarian at the now defunct Jardín Gaia Wildlife Rescue Center in Manuel Antonio. On the third day she took it to Jardín Gaia, where they cared for it until it reached an age when it could be reintroduced into the wild. They eventually released it in a rainforest near the Savegre River.

"How does Jack decide whether to be cruel or kind?" Or maybe you asked, "Why does he hate sloths and pelicans, and love hawks and anteaters?"

It's really not that much of a puzzle. The baby sloth had fallen for some reason unknown to us. Maybe it had a genetic defect. Maybe it was sick and too weak to hang on. The important thing is that its mother had no interest in retrieving it. Mother sloths seldom try to rescue fallen young, because what is good for the individual may not be good for the species. Defective or weak individuals don't survive to reproduce, and their defective genes are not passed on to offspring. The unwritten rule for baby three-toed sloths *(Bradypus variegatus)* is this: If you can't hang on to Mom by yourself we don't want you perpetuating our species. Get your butt out of our gene pool. Harsh, you say? Yes, but it keeps the species fit.

The raptor was a little different. Its misfortune was caused by humans. Nature didn't put barbed wire in the double-toothed kite's habitat, humans did. I figured that since it was my fence that the hawk got hung up on, it was my responsibility to do what I could to remedy the situation. Fortunately the damage was only minor, and the young predator lived to hunt again, maybe even to prey on baby sloths.

With the pelican we're back to Mother Nature again. Humans did nothing to break the bird's wing. This type of misfortune befalls pelicans frequently. Over the years, I have seen several pelicans with broken wings. The bird might have been old or undernourished or even had the avian equivalent of osteoporosis. Maybe it was just an unlucky accident. The point is that Mother Nature determined that the individual in question should perish, and who am I to argue with Mother Nature? If Diane had been awake when Shirley brought it by the house, I'd probably still be buying fish for that unfortunate pelican. By having returned it to the beach it served a purpose in nature by becoming food for crabs and vultures.

In the case of the anteater, the damage was done by a domestic dog, someone's pet. Additionally I believe the man who brought it to me was mistaken. I don't believe that a dog could have fatally injured a mother anteater *(Tamandua mexicana)*. Usually, it is the dog that gets ripped open by the anteater. The anteater rolls onto its back, and when the dog goes for the kill, the anteater digs its long, curved claws into the flesh of the dog's face and neck, and slashes. The anteater remains on its back in this defensive posture until the dog leaves. I believe that the man saw the mother tamandua in this position and mistakenly thought that she was near death. So he picked up the baby, lying a short distance away, and brought it to me, thinking he was saving its life. Mother Nature didn't put misfortune in the baby tamandua's way. It was a human pet that caused the incident, and this was probably compounded by human error. Nature wasn't dictating the death sentence on this youngster, human beings were. Fortunately, we were able to save it and return it to its natural habitat.

We hear a lot about animal rights these days. In the wild, animals don't have rights. They are born in a highly competitive environment where only the very fittest survive. All have an opportunity to fight for survival, nothing more. Animals that die aren't lost. They become food for other living things. Their bodies are consumed by predators and scavengers, insects, fungi and bacteria. They are broken down into basic elements for reuse. The nutrients are all cycled back into the ecosystem and are assimilated by other plants and animals. We've all heard the term "food chain." I think that "nutrient cycle" would be more appropriate. The most important lesson the rainforest has for us is that every living thing sooner or later becomes food for some other living thing. That even includes us.

If you find an injured animal you may wish to apply this criteria to the case. The most important thing to remember is that when you take in a wild animal, you and only you are responsible for it. Don't expect someone else to take it off your hands, and don't try to dump it in someone else's lap. Also, you should keep in mind that it is illegal to keep a wild animal in captivity without a permit, even if in your view you are helping it. If you decide to care for the animal and try to get it into a rescue center, keep in mind that rescue centers are all overburdened with wildlife and are drastically under funded. They are very appreciative of any financial help you can provide when you take the animal to them. Caring for wildlife is expensive, and the only funding these places receive comes from donations. ᑐ

Chapter 24
Those Dangerous Eco-Nuts

On the southern Pacific coast of Costa Rica at the point where the Barú River empties into the sea there is a town called Dominical. Near the river in a swampy area where nobody has yet figured out how to build a house live Ma and Pa Skeeter and Lil Skeeter. One day Pa, perched on a twig with Lil, was recounting the great triumphs of the Skeeter clan.

"I tell ya, Lil, us Skeeters hez been aroun fer bout a hunert millyun years, an we's got a hist'ry ta be proud uv. Who wud think thet anythin ez tiny ez us'ns cud cause so much havoc fer them *Homo sapiens*? Ya know, Lil, us Skeeters kin claim credit fer killin more uv them humans then eny other species. Not tigers ner bears ner sharks ner crocodiles, not even them poisonous snakes kin claim ez many kills."

"Wow, Pa, thet's awesome!"

"Even more, Lil. I bet we done kilt more then all uv them others put together. We may be lil', but we packs a pow'rful biological wallop. Ar species kin carry malaria an yellow fever from one uv them humans ta nother, an jus malaria done kilt more people then eny other disease, over a millyun a year fer more years then you kin count. Thet's even more'n they done kilt uv each other in all ther crazy wars put together."

"But Pa, ain't them humans s'posed ta be smart? Why don't they do sumpin bout us Skeeters? Kin't they hurt us?"

"Well, Lil, they is s'posed ta be smart, but fer bein smart they shur duz dumb thins. Like one time they even thot they wuz gonna exterminate us Skeeters. They invented this stuff they calls DDT an spread it all over thuh place. Sure, they kilt a bunch uv us'ns, but thuh ones they kilt wuz thuh weakest. An, not only thet, but they kilt off a whole mess uv ar enemies, ya know, like birds, bats, frogs, geckos, fish, spiders, dragonflies an all kines uv other stuff thet eats us Skeeters. They even poisont ther-selves with thet DDT stuff, imagine thet! But then without no enemies we came back strong. I mean, when yer Ma lays eggs, she lays lots uv eggs, an when there ain't no fish in thuh swamps ta eat ar larva an there ain't no frogs in thuh puddles ta eat ar young'uns an all them birds an bats cain't reperduce so well cuz thuh poisons dun messed up ther innards, well, I'll tell ya, Lil, them wuz thuh days."

"Listen, Pa," interjected Ma Skeeter, "I's gonna go git a meal ta-night cuz I needs ta lay a mess uv eggs ta-morrow. Why don't ya come long an bring Lil, cuz someday soon she's gonna have ta suck blood an lay eggs, too. We'll show er how it's done an maybe spread a lil' dengue er encephalitis while wer et it."

"Great i-dee, Ma. How bout it, Lil?"

"Gee, Ma an Pa, cud I? That'ud be so so-o-o-o coo-o-o-ol. But, Pa, is them humans still poisonin everthin with thet ther DDT?"

"Naw, Lil, now they's got worse stuff, an they sprays it out uv flyin machines they calls air-o-planes. Ya see, they thinks thet they is thuh only critters on this planet what counts an thet they kin jus kill anythin else thet eats thuh same stuff they eats. So when sompin else wants a bite uv thuh plants them humans eats, well they flies aroun in one uv them air-o-planes an sprays poisons all over thuh place. Then it's like Skeeter heaven. All them frogs an fish an spiders an geckos an all them other nasty thins dies, but we kin reperduce so fast thet thuh ones uv us thet survives has it real easy an then we's immune ta them poisons. An not only thet, but them humans is still poisonin ther-selves with all thet stuff. It gits in ther water an ther food. Kin ya think uv anything so dumb as ta put poison on sompin ya's'gonna eat er drink? They evun has thuh stuff in cans ta spray it all over ther houses. Unbuhlievable!"

"Yeh, Pa, I sees whut ya means. But, Pa, I hears they's a'tryin ta git rid uv us Skeeters by gittin rid uv all thuh places wher we breeds."

"Ha! Did ya see all thuh trash on thuh beach after thet ther Holy Week they calls *Semana Santa*? Us Skeeters kin breed in anythin thet holds water, even a bottle cap. Them humans left anuff breedin places aroun fer us Skeeters ta perduce millyuns an millyuns uv young'uns. They talks bout cleanin up ther own waste, but ther's always enough trash layin aroun fer us ta breed in."

"Hey, Pa, gether up Lil. Lets git goin. It's gittin dark an it's startin ta rain. Jus perfect fer a blood feast."

"Wow, Ma an Pa, this is gonna be so coo-o-ol."

The Skeeter family sets off along the edge of the wetland, flying close to the ground through the low-lying vegetation. They pass by several houses with varying amounts of litter outside and eventually come to one with lots of plants and trees, but no trash.

"Let's go in here, Pa," says Ma. "We don wanna spread no diseases ta thuh people thet leaves lots uv breedin places fer us Skeeters, but this here house looks like thuh kind uv human we kin do without. Lil, you remember thet when you's old enough."

"Awright, Ma. But let's go in. I wants ta see ya suck thet blood."

The Skeeters look for a way to enter and quickly find a crack where they can crawl through to the inside.

"Look, Pa, they's a'sleepin, an they ain't got no Skeeter net. This is gonna be easy pickins."

"Hey, Pa, what's a Path uv thuh Tapir Biological Corridor?"

"What you talkin bout, Lil. Wher you hear bout thet?"

"Right on this here T-shirt a'hangin on this here chair, Pa. See?"

"Oh, shee-it! Look here, Ma. This place must buhlong ta one uv them weirdo ecologists. They prob'ly don't use no poisons. This place is prob'ly jus crawlin with frogs, an geckos an all sorts uv scary stuff. Some uv these places has even got bats an spiderwebs. These eco-nuts is dangerous. We better haul ass. You know how many uv us Skeeters one bat kin gobble up in one night?"

"Rivit, rrrrri-i-ivet."

"What thuh hell wuz thet?"

"Rivit, rivet—kerwhap-slurp."

"Pa, Pa, where's you et?"

"Rivit, rivit, rrrri-i-i-ivet—kerwhap-slurp. Rrrri-ivet, rrrrri-i-i-ivet—kerwhap-slurp."

The Path of the Tapir Biological Corridor, under the leadership of ASANA, proposes to restore natural habitat and natural balance and help people to live in harmony with their environment. ⟳

Chapter 25

Close Encounters in the Slow Lane

The first whiff of danger drifted lightly into the nostrils of the sleeping furry bundle, penetrating the fog of slumber. A moment later the tree limb where it clung wiggled, triggering it instantly into a full state of alertness. Adrenaline flowed into its veins as it moved quickly toward the relative safety of the flimsy end of the branch. But a perica ligera *moving quickly isn't much of a match for a* tolomuco. *The first of the three sleek, black predators caught the slow-moving mammal just before it reached the point where the tree limb tapered sharply. Twice the size of a large house cat, the* tolomuco *clung to the thicker part of the branch with its rear claws while it reached out to rake its front claws across the back leg of the* perica ligera. *One of the* tolomuco's *companions was on another branch off to one side trying in vain to reach the prey, while the other was almost directly underneath.*

Pain penetrated its flesh as the perica ligera *pulled free, then took another laborious step toward the end of the branch and out of reach of its pursuer. With the next step the thin tip of the branch dropped suddenly and the* perica ligera, *which was hanging upside down, found itself nearer the tormentor waiting below. But the slow mover knew where it wanted to be, and its only hope of survival was to keep moving. The lower* tolomuco *almost lost its balance as it reached upward and took a swipe at the prey's head, catching the lower jaw with a claw. Blood oozed from the gash, but the pain only brought more adrenaline and onward went the* perica ligera *to the leafy end of the branch. Abruptly it dropped completely past the perch of the predator and the* perica ligera *reached out, stretching its arm to the limit, and grasped a thin woody vine with both of the long, curved, blunt claws. The thick nails closed tightly on the vine, and the blonde, furry bundle released its grip on the branch. Its heart was pounding, but onward it went, knowing without looking that its agile enemies were racing for new positions. Hanging underneath the vine it moved forward foot over hand, hand over foot. Sanctuary was in sight when two swift swipes came unexpectedly. The first opened a deep wound across its face and the second raked its shoulder but didn't penetrate its hairy coat or hide. Another black demon was moving into position on the side. One more foot forward and then a hand, and the vine dipped almost straight down. The terrified animal half slid while trying to reach the bottom of the loop where the woody vine curved back up and into the branches of another tree. At last it breathed heavily, grasping the vine with all four feet. Now it could rest, securely out of reach of its pursuers.*

The three *tolomucos* looked down when they heard the human voice. "Look, look, up there! See them? They're tayras. Wait a minute, look out there on the vine, it's a sloth. This one is different than the other one we saw; this is a two-toed sloth."

A mixture of voices came from the people. "Pedro, look. The sloth is bleeding. What happened? Did those cats hurt it?"

"Those are tayras, not cats," explained the veteran Hacienda Barú guide. "They're like weasels. It looks like they were trying kill the sloth, but it got out on that vine. It can grasp the thin vine, but the tayras can't hold on with their claws."

For almost a half-hour the group of visitors watched, mesmerized, as the tayras tried unsuccessfully to reach the sloth. Finally the people moved on, feeling privileged to have witnessed such an amazing spectacle.

People often ask which animals prey on sloths. Their traditional predator was the harpy eagle *(Harpia harpyja)*, now near extinction. When this large raptor was common, it was known to snatch sloths from their arboreal perches. The crested eagle *(Morphnus guianensis)*, ornate hawk-eagle *(Spizaetus ornatus)*, and black hawk-eagle *(Spizaetus tyrannus)* are all known to take opossums and kinkajous, sloth-size mammals, from the canopy, and are certainly capable of killing sloths as well. The white hawk *(Leucopternis albicollis)* and some of the other large hawks are known to grab baby sloths from their mothers, but would have difficulty with an adult. Since Pedro's experience proves that tayras *(Eira barbara)* prey on sloths, it is almost certain that ocelots and margay cats prey on them as well. Additionally, a large boa constrictor could easily kill and swallow a full grown sloth. Nevertheless, none of these predators are a major threat to either the Hoffman's two-toed sloth *(Choloepus hoffmanni)*, known locally as the *perica ligera* or the brown-throated, three-toed sloth *(Bradypus variegatus)*, commonly called the *cucula*. Attacks are probably infrequent and have little effect on the population.

Both species of sloth are considered threatened and are protected by the Costa Rican Wildlife Protection Law #7317 and are listed in Appendix II and III of the CITES international wildlife protection treaty. Presumably because of their leafy diet, sloth meat is not normally consumed by humans, and therefore hunting isn't a menace. Habitat destruction is the foremost threat to their continued existence. Fortunately, secondary forest cover is increasing in the area around Dominical, as property owners continue to plant trees and allow former pastures to return to their natural forested state. These acts increase habitat and food supply for sloths, and their population here is increasing.

The sloth's slow manner gives the impression of laziness, and the word for sloth in many if not all languages means lazy. According to the book of lists, *The Top 10 of Everything*, by Russell Ash, sloths sleep about twenty hours per day, placing them second only to the koala in the rankings for the world's laziest animals.

Considering the sloth's reputation for slothfulness, it is rather ironic that they have a record of arriving first. Eight million years ago, when geological forces were forming Central America, the first South American mammals to set foot on the isthmus were two species of ground sloth that had to swim over 60 kilometers (37 miles) of treacherous ocean to reach the new land. They won the race five million years ahead of four other species of sloths and many other mammals that arrived later. At Hacienda Barú National Wildlife Refuge when we started restoring natural forest habitat to land formerly used for crops and pasture, the sloths appeared in these corridors after a few short years, when the new trees were still quite small. A 2001 issue of *The Dominical Current* newspaper had a photo of a sloth in Dominical across the street from San Clemente in an area that was deforested over fifty years ago. That land had been regenerating into secondary growth for less than ten years. Wherever suitable habitat exists the sloths will soon arrive.

Personally, I find sloths enchanting. There is something so special and friendly about them that it is hard to describe. I sometimes guide visitors into the tops of rainforest trees where these charismatic mammals reside, and occasionally find myself in close proximity to them. I call these experiences *Close Encounters in the Slow Lane*. Each is different, yet all have a certain magical quality that makes them unforgettable.

In one such experience we first saw the grayish-colored animal climbing steadily up a thick, woody vine called a liana. Dan, Philipa and I were hanging in the crown of a large rainforest tree, about as high off the ground as a twelve-story building. We watched the slow-moving mammal off and on as it advanced lazily but steadily.

After ten minutes its path was obvious. Still over 10 meters (33 feet) beneath us, it was working its way up through the tangle of vines and branches, clearly heading our way. Elated by the possibility of a close encounter, we watched intently as it emerged from a mass of foliage and continued upward. The long, powerful claws of the three-toed sloth or *cucula* became clearly visible as it moved hand over hand up the thick woody stem, carefully grasping and testing each new hold before releasing the previous one.

The sloth neared the large branch of a strangler fig *(Ficus spp.)*, which was attached to the giant camarón tree *(Licania operculipetala)* in which we were suspended. It turned slightly, giving us a view of its back. The long hair and thin black stripe running down the spine indicated that it was a female; males have a swath of short hair there, with a wide black stripe surrounded by brownish-orange hair. We could see a faint greenish tint to her coat as she passed right in front of us, less than 3 meters (10 feet) away, then briefly disappeared behind the trunk of the fig.

Our next view came when the crown of her head eased over the top of the large fig branch and she stared straight into our eyes, a surprised look on her face. At first she was quite coy, occasionally ducking behind the branch in a slow-motion game of peek-a-boo. All of her movements were like molasses in January, even eye blinks. After nearly five minutes of looking us over and, I imagine, considering her alternatives, the young female made her decision. Unhurriedly she pulled herself over the top of the branch and inched her way down the woody vine on our side of the fig.

"Don't let her grab your leg," I whispered to Dan, who was dangling almost directly in her path. Dan shifted slightly, but left his foot on the liana.

No one spoke. We could clearly see the moss clinging to her hair and the flies and beetles moving through it. I felt a strange closeness, an affinity with this charismatic denizen of the rainforest canopy. Any of us could have reached out and touched this beautiful young female as she slowly traversed the few meters from the fig branch to her next obstacle, Dan's foot. I held my breath as she contemplated it for a moment, reached out with her right hand, pushed his foot out of the way with a surprisingly brusque movement, then continued onward. I relaxed but didn't stop watching as she followed the path of the liana down a short distance to where it looped around and came back up, bringing her to a point near Philipa. The sloth continued steadily on over to the far side of the tree and the young, tender strangler fig leaves that were her objective. After only a couple of mouthfuls she went to sleep, apparently exhausted from her long climb. The whole journey took her 45 minutes, during which she traveled about 50 meters (165 feet).

Encounters like these are so emotionally intense that the feeling is difficult to describe. I usually find myself in the canopy of Hacienda Barú National Wildlife Refuge a couple of times each week and touching distance from a sloth about three times each year. I never get bored with these episodes. Each time is as exhilarating as the last. I'm thankful that I have the opportunity to know these captivating animals on such an intimate basis. With each encounter, I feel a little closer to them. Sometimes I recognize sloths as individuals, and it seems like I'm meeting an old friend. Regardless, each *close encounter in the slow lane* is magical and something to be treasured. ⌒

Chapter 26

Carrying Things to Extremes: Extremely Beautiful, Extremely Toxic

*W*hat in the world do you suppose that frog is doing all the *way up here*, I thought. Ten meters (33 feet) below, the bright green spot inched its way up the trunk. I could barely determine that it was a frog, even with binoculars. Over the next half-hour its progress brought it to my level in the crown of a giant rainforest tree, about as high as a ten-story building. The coloration indicated that it was a green and black poison dart frog *(Dendrobates auratus)* commonly found in the tropical forests of Costa Rica. Having reached the upper branches, the frog proceeded to explore its surroundings, hopping along the thick limbs and trunk. Now that its meandering was horizontal rather than vertical, *Dendrobates* was able to cover more distance with the same amount of effort. At one point during its travels, the frog passed less than an arm's length from where I was dangling from a rope in my climbing harness. Its pattern of movement was typical of the species, several hops followed by a brief rest. The pauses gave me an opportunity for a closer look. The brightly-colored frog, about the size of a large butter bean, sported brilliant green splotches on a coal black background. Its smooth skin glistened in the soft light of the forest.

Looking closely, I hoped to find a tadpole attached to its back, but none was there.

The males of *Dendrobates auratus* are known to carry tadpoles one at a time to aerial locations such as hollows in branches and trunks where deposits of water provide a medium where the young may live and mature. Epiphytic plants called bromeliads that capture and retain water are a common place for this. The green and black dart frog, however, is not known to take its tadpoles more than 20 meters (65 feet) into the trees, and we were 35 meters (115 feet) above the rainforest floor. Had there been a tadpole stuck to the adult's back, it would have been a first. With some species of *Dendrobates*, the female will visit the site where the male leaves the tadpoles and deposit infertile eggs in the water as food for the offspring. Tadpoles of the green and black dart frog are not so fortunate and don't receive a free handout. They have to make it on their own, scrounging algae, detritus and insect larvae in order to grow and mature. They have even been known to eat each other, especially when there is a significant size difference amongst the siblings.

Dart frog folklore is fascinating because of their extreme toxicity. Although most amphibians are toxic to one extent or another, these brightly colored frogs go to extremes. Within the category of poison dart frogs, *Dendrobates* could be classified as moderately toxic, meaning that touching one will not cause any ill effects unless it is done repeatedly. Members of another genera, *Phyllobates*, are dangerous to the touch. They are known to be some of the most toxic animals in the world. In fact, a species found in the Choco region of Colombia, *Phyllobates terribilis*, is listed by *Guinness Book of World Records* as the most poisonous animal on earth, and *A Guide to Amphibians and Reptiles of Costa Rica*, by Twan Leenders tells us that its skin contains a toxin which is "...the strongest animal toxin known to biologists." According to Leenders, one of these tiny yellow frogs carries enough nerve toxin to kill ten adult human beings.

The Choco tribal people use the toxin on their blow gun darts. Some sources say they do this by pinning the frog to the ground with a sharp stick while they touch the darts to its skin. Others say that a member of the tribe uses a very long fingernail to hold the frog securely by pressing down on one of its feet. The hunters then pass by one-by-one and touch the points of their darts to its skin. The frog is then released unharmed to produce more poison for future hunts. So powerful is the toxin that a mere prick from the dart will cause the prey to enter into a state of paralysis and die.

Many years ago, a researcher who was studying *Phyllobates terribilis* dart frogs in the Choco of Colombia became quite ill. Knowing only that his health was deteriorating, the biologist grew concerned and finally flew back to the United States, where he consulted with top tropical medicine specialists. Nobody seemed able to diagnose his condition, and none of the recommended medical treatments worked. Although not disabled, the biologist was definitely ill and worsening. In desperation he flew back to Colombia and returned to the area where he had been working. The tribal people recognized his symptoms as those of dart frog poisoning and offered to make an antidote from rainforest herbs. After a week of treatment with the tribal remedy the scientist's health returned to normal. Having always worn plastic gloves as a precaution when handling the brightly colored amphibians, the biologist had felt certain that his condition was not related to the frogs. But apparently his mere proximity to *Phyllobates terribilis* on a daily basis was sufficient to affect his health.

The bright coloration of the dart frogs is like an advertisement to potential predators. It's like the frog is saying: "See my bright colors? If you eat me, you die!" Even in nature, however, mistakes are made. Naturalist guide Deiner Cascante had been taking ecological travelers into the rainforest of Hacienda Barú National Wildlife Refuge for fourteen years. In that time he had never seen any animal show the slightest interest in dart frogs. Then one day, he and a group of visitors sighted a venomous snake called a *terciopelo* alongside a small stream. It was coiled and alert. A short distance in front of the viper's head, a green and black poison dart frog, startled by the hikers, hopped from behind a stone. The snake struck, and both of its fangs passed completely through the frog. Shaking its head violently, the serpent dislodged the small amphibian, which dropped to the ground and hopped away, injured but still mobile. Deiner thinks that the snake was nervous about the approaching group of people and had its attention riveted on this potential threat. When *Dentrobates* suddenly entered its field of vision, the *terciopelo* struck reflexively, without being fully aware of what it was biting. Upon realizing its error, the snake immediately took measures to rid itself of this tiny package of poison. During the few minutes that the people observed the two poisonous animals after the incident, neither showed any sign of intoxication.

One research report indicates that two species of an attractive rainforest bird called the motmot eat the green and black dart frog and suffer no apparent ill effects. This is a splendid example of how Mother Nature has developed defenses in some of her creatures against substances that baffle modern science. Modern medicine was helpless against the toxin that affected the scientist in Colombia. Yet, the tribal people, using only products from the rainforest, were able to cure him. Nature contains a vast databank with more stored information than all the libraries on earth. This alone is sufficient reason to protect the few remaining rainforests on our planet.

Other mysteries surrounding the dart frogs relate to what it eats, rather than what eats it. Hacienda Barú guide Pedro Porras once noticed about a dozen of the green and black amphibians hopping around on a dead branch that was lying on the rainforest floor. The rotting wood was covered with a white, fluffy mushroom that the frogs appeared to be eating. Never having seen so many at once and thinking that their diet was made up entirely of insects, Pedro was confused by the incident. The next day there were no mushrooms on the dead branch and no frogs. A few days later, Pedro passed by the same place in the morning and the branch was bare, but in the afternoon the mushrooms had again materialized and so had the frogs. As the visitors that Pedro was guiding took photos of the spectacle, the naturalist guide moved in for a closer look. As it turned out, the mushrooms, which appeared on the trunk for a short time and then disappeared like magic, were attracting swarms of small black gnats that the frogs were gobbling up, just like a bunch of kids tearing into their Halloween candy.

Unraveling the mysteries of the dart frogs is fascinating work. One problem scientists are trying to solve is how these powerful toxins may be used by humans in the manufacture of painkillers. Another unsolved mystery is why the frog has evolved such extreme toxicity. What possible ecological advantage could enough toxin to kill a dozen or more adult humans give to a tiny yellow frog like *Phyllobates terribilis*? One-hundredth or even one-thousandth of this extreme level of toxicity would certainly be sufficient to deter predators. To my knowledge nobody understands why the dart frogs are so poisonous, but biologists are learning a little about how the frogs make their toxins.

The first clue came from the discovery that dart frogs of all species lose their toxicity when kept in captivity in a terrarium. Suspecting that a variation from their natural diet might be the cause, biologists began to pay close attention to what the colorful amphibians eat in the wild. It turned out that a high percentage of their natural prey was ants. In fact, the least toxic genera of dart frogs, *Colostethus*, consumes the fewest ants, while the extremely poisonous *Phyllobates* eats them almost exclusively. Moderately toxic *Dendrobates* is somewhere in between, with a diet containing 50 to 70 percent ants. Knowing that ants tend to contain a high level of alkaloids and that dart frog toxins are primarily alkaloids, biologists have come to the conclusion that these amazing frogs have "learned" how to concentrate the alkaloids that they acquire from eating ants in the toxic mucous secreted through glands in their skin. In the case of *Phyllobates terribilis*, the toxin is so powerful that, according to *Guinness Book of World Records*, ten-millionths of a gram will kill an adult human being. If the *Guinness* figure is correct, one drop of pure *Phyllobates terribilis* toxin would be enough to kill 5,000 people. The amount of toxin in the skin of one of the tiny yellow frogs is much less than a drop.

This is all quite fascinating, but none of it explains what my green and black dart frog was doing 35 meters above the forest floor in the crown of a rainforest tree. To better understand the magnitude of this feat we need to keep in mind that the frog was only about 35 millimeters (less than 1½ inches) long. To climb 35 meters means it climbed 1,000 times its own body length. To put this in perspective, let's imagine a person of average height, 1.8 meters (5 feet, 10 inches) climbing a stairway 1,000 times his or her own height. That person would have to climb to 1.8 kilometers (just over one mile) above the surface of the earth! It would be like ascending a stairway to the top of five Empire State Buildings of 102 stories each or six Eiffel Towers stacked on top of each other. This feat would have to be accomplished in two hours. Not only that, but the frog didn't have any stairs to climb. It went straight up the side of the tree trunk. I don't know what *Dendrobates* was doing up there, but it must have been pretty important. ∾

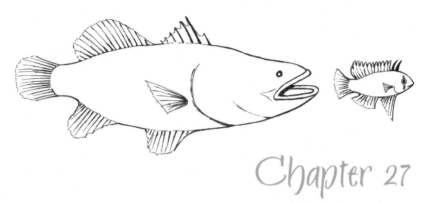

Chapter 27

Alien Invasion:
Exotics, Non-Natives and Invasives

*T*he first ones were garbage eaters. They lived near the bottom in the shallow water, feeding on bits of organic debris and rotting pieces of dead plants and animals. They were the scavengers of the muddy bottom. At some point in time one was born with a difference in its mouth parts; its teeth were a little flatter. There were so many others competing for the rotten debris that the new one often went hungry, until one day, driven by hunger pangs, it ate something new: living algae. It thrived on the new source of nutrients, as did its young. There came a time when the water rose, adding new nooks, crannies and rocks to its habitat. Then again one appeared with altered mouth parts; this time it was larger lips. The lips weren't the best for eating algae and besides there was less algae in the water now. One day it saw a small ripple in the surface and reflexively snapped at the movement, grasping an insect that fell there. With time it got better at catching live insects, and it grew and reproduced. Over many generations the lips grew even thicker, eyes grew sharper and the body longer and slimmer allowing for quick movement. These were the insect-catching and -eating specialists.

Back near the bottom, one of its ancestors bore an offspring with upturned mouth and large, hard-rounded teeth. It learned to feed on snails. Later its offspring and their offspring learned to feed on other shelled animals. Selective pressures assured that the best fitted to find and crush the shelled prey were the most likely to survive and reproduce. At the same time, one of the fat-lipped insect eaters with slightly sharper teeth began to eat the young of the others. And even later another learned to catch and eat the larger plant-eaters. Only the individuals best suited for acquiring and consuming their own special type of food survived and reproduced. The others either branched off and found a new specialty or perished, never to pass on their genes.

This simplified tale illustrates how, over thousands of years, as the waters of the lake rose, more specialized niches developed, and with each new habitat and each new source of food one of the cichlids "learned" how to occupy the space and eat the nutrient source. Over 200,000 years elapsed until one day in 1858 an explorer named John Hanning Speke became the first European to behold the giant lake. Being a loyal British subject, Speke named Lake Victoria in honor of the queen. At that time it was nearly twice as big as Costa Rica, with a shoreline that would stretch halfway around the earth. But the most amazing thing about the lake was the 500 different species of cichlid fish that filled it from top to bottom and shore to shore, utilizing every way imaginable to make a living in that enormous body of water. Almost all of them evolved from a single ancestral species.

Then one day some European sport fishermen decided that the lake needed a good game fish. It was no fun to catch all the "trash fish" that the locals fished for food. So they released a non-native species called the Nile perch, a real sport fish, into Lake Victoria. Now they had a fish that was fun to catch, a strong fighter that could reach the length of a tall man and twice the weight. A voracious eater, the perch ate its way through the cichlids like a hungry young boy in a cookie jar. In half a century the Nile perch has eaten over 200 species of Lake Victoria cichlids into extinction. The algae eaters were some of the first to disappear, and possibly none of them are left. Lake Victoria became choked with algae, which consumes much of the oxygen, leaving less for the fish and causing many to die. The rotting plant material accumulated and the decomposition process took even more oxygen, and soon the bottom-feeders died too. Later the shallow portions of the lake became choked with water hyacinth, another non-native species, this one from the Amazon. The thick mats of broad pads of this invasive species are so dense that local fishermen can't force their boats through them. Malaria carrying mosquitos breed in them as does a snail that carries a terrible parasite called *Bilharzia*. Three million people who live around the lake have been deprived of their livelihood, and it all began with the introduction of the Nile perch. Lake Victoria has been called the worst ecological disaster of our time.

According to *World Book Encyclopedia*: "Invasive species are animals, plants and other living things that spread rapidly in new environments where there are few or no natural controls on their growth." When a given species remains in the habitat where it evolved over many millennia, there are many other species that have evolved together with it. Some of them prey on it, some of them compete with it for food or space, and some of them will parasitize it or make it ill. In turn, each of those species have others that keep them in check. When a species is removed from its native environment and placed in a strange habitat within its preferred range of temperature, humidity and altitude, there are often few, if any, other species that can keep it under control. That's when the problems begin.

We are all familiar with invasive species, even though we may not know it. If you live in the United States, you are certainly familiar with European starlings, the black birds that clutter up many public parks; kudzu, a broad-leafed vine that chokes out native vegetation and takes over vast areas; purple loosestrife, zebra mussels, Dutch elm disease or West Nile fever. If you're from Australia you know about European rabbits or the Madagascar rubber vine. If you're British you may know about the flatworms from New Zealand that are rapidly consuming all of the country's earthworms, so important for building and enhancing the soil.

In the example of the Nile perch in Lake Victoria, the invasive species caused major ecological damage by preying directly on native species to the point of driving many to extinction. The kudzu vine out-competes native species and crowds them out of their space. The European rabbits in Australia multiplied rapidly and consumed pasture that humans need for sheep production. Some invasives bring diseases, like the mosquitos that carry malaria and yellow fever or the rats whose fleas carry bubonic plague. Still others interbreed with native species, altering them genetically. An example of this latter would be the so-called killer bees that accidentally got established in Brazil and worked their way north arriving in the southern United States about a decade later. They interbred with local honey bees everywhere they went, to the point that none of the original pure bloodlines were left.

Often when a non-native species arrives at a new location, it will alter one thing in the environment and that, in turn, will alter other aspects of the environment in a domino effect. In his excellent book on the subject, *Life Out of Bounds*, Chris Bright recounts the story of the opossum shrimp in the Flathead River in Montana:

> "Wildlife officials introduced the shrimp around 1970 to increase the forage base for the kokanee salmon, another introduced species. But salmon tend to feed near the surface and the shrimp only rose to the surface at night, when the salmon could not see them. So the salmon could not eat the shrimp, but the shrimp ate all the plankton that the salmon

fry depended on. The salmon population crashed, then the bears, birds of prey, and other creatures that had come to depend on the salmon disappeared. A tiny shrimp had starved eagles out of the sky."

To my knowledge we haven't had any disasters resulting from bioinvasions in Costa Rica, though we do have some non-native species that have the potential to cause problems. We have thousands of hectares of melina plantations that were planted for paper pulp. A number of imported pasture grasses tend to take over and are extremely difficult to get rid of. One in particular, German grass, tends to cover wetlands and form thick mats that soak up all the water and crowd out waterbirds. However, I've noticed that where there is a large native forest nearby, these grasses eventually tend to choke themselves out and, with time, native trees will repopulate the area. In the tropics there are many more species and a lot more competition than in temperate climates, which makes it more difficult for exotics to become established. This large variety of species is called biodiversity, and it is the key to a healthy environment. That doesn't mean the tropics are safe, by any means. Lake Victoria sits on the equator in east central Africa. It does mean that we need to seriously protect our biodiversity.

The Costa Rican environmental ministry, MINAE, with the enthusiastic assistance of many environmental organizations, has elaborated a strategy for the conservation of the biodiversity of Costa Rica. Additionally, there is a plan for each conservation area within the country. You can find these on the Internet at *www.minae.go.cr/estrategia*. Protecting our biodiversity is the best thing we can do to defend ourselves against invasive species. Altered habitats are more vulnerable than intact ones. We need to conserve our tropical forests.

We have a multitude of beautiful native plants in Costa Rica, some flowering, some useful and others merely decorative. If you live in Costa Rica, when you go to a nursery to buy plants for your garden or for landscaping your new home, tell them you want species native to Costa Rica. Better yet, buy from local people. Many country people love plants and have elaborate gardens. They often pot and sell some of their more attractive ones. These are usually displayed by placing the potted plants out by the roadside where motorists will see them and stop to browse and hopefully purchase some. That way you will not only be protecting biodiversity, you will also be helping the local people.

Just because Costa Rica hasn't experienced a disaster on the scale of Lake Victoria doesn't mean we don't have to be on guard. There are some critters out there that could really wreak havoc here. Let's have a little fun and invent our own nightmare: an animal that, if introduced into Costa Rica, could upset the entire country, not just ecologically, but economically and socially as well. Something that would strike terror into the hearts of everyone, drive away the tourists, destroy fauna and leave the country in a shambles. What characteristics would this imaginary demon have?

First of all, it must be small enough to stow away on a ship or plane without detection and hardy enough to survive a long journey without food. Since one is not enough to invade a country, reproduce and establish a population capable of becoming a threat, more than one should be able to travel on the same vessel, or they should be adept enough to stow away many different times. Let's say it is very sneaky, not easily detected and has a knack for slipping into homes, hotel rooms, offices and just about anywhere it wants to go. Since people are terrified of poisonous animals let's make it poisonous enough to kill people, especially smaller children and pets. It won't have any natural predators and will tend to prey on some of our most treasured wildlife.

So what do you think? Does our fantasy animal sound terrifying enough? I hate to tell you this, but this thing isn't imaginary; it really exists. The brown tree snake, a native of Asia, was introduced into Guam during World War II. It is not known exactly how it arrived on Guam, but it probably came in a cargo ship's hold. What is known is that they have driven twelve of Guam's fourteen bird species to extinction, destroyed the tourist industry and created paranoia in other Pacific islands, especially Hawaii, where several of them have been discovered in the wheel wells of jet planes. The brown tree snake is poisonous enough to kill a child and has a nasty habit of sneaking into dwellings and small spaces. They are excellent climbers, and their long slender bodies can reach 3 meters (almost 10 feet) in length. This species has another trait that makes it the nightmare invader: After a female mates, possibly with several different males, she carries the sperm within her body and may not fertilize the ova and bear young until six months to a year later; and she can have several sets of offspring from one mating. So, conceivably, one impregnated female, stowed away in a ship's cargo hold and off-loaded with the cargo, would be sufficient to populate Costa Rica. One of them was once found inside a new washing machine that was manufactured in Korea, off-loaded in Guam, loaded on another boat and shipped to Houston, where it was discovered.

The worst incident ever was a brown tree snake that found its way into a septic tank, probably through the ventilation tube. It crawled up the tube that discharges waste from the toilet into the septic tank, and, you guessed it, bit someone who was sitting on the toilet. I know not where it bit them. Sound scary enough? Chances are the brown tree snake won't make it to Costa Rica, but it's possible and there are plenty of other scary things out there as well. Be careful with exotics. Stick with natives. Let's protect our biodiversity. ∿

Chapter 28

Hateful Devils the Ants Won't Even Eat

I used to shoot them. We all knew they were evil. My friend Chepo told me he would shoot them any time he found them on his farm. "They're so bad," he told me, "that nothing will eat them, not even the ants." We all knew it was illegal, but we did it anyway and felt entirely justified in doing so. I mean, how could anyone justify protecting something so evil that it will eat a live baby as it is being born, emerging from its mother's womb? Sometimes they get so excited in their feeding frenzy that they even eat the mother's vulva and teats when she is flat on her side and can't stand up because of the birth contractions. When they find any helpless creature down on the ground they pluck out its eyes, eat its tongue, nose, anus and udder, even before it's dead. Now, many years later, I realize that everything has its place in nature; everything plays its role in the ecological balance, regardless of how hateful its natural habits may seem to us. I don't even hate them anymore.

It almost seems like a past life back in the 1970s and early 1980s when we raised cattle on Hacienda Barú. Large numbers of vultures were a common sight soaring on the thermals above the cow herds, especially at calving time when there was plenty to eat. We didn't mind them cleaning up the placentas left from the calving cows, but the scenario described above was all too frequent, and most cattlemen killed vultures in one way or another. If you shoot them whenever they come around, the vultures become wary and tend to keep a little more distance from the livestock. They learn quickly.

Of the four species of vultures found in Costa Rica, two are a common sight in the skies over Dominical: the turkey vulture *(Cathartes aura)* and the black vulture *(Coragyps atratus)*. A third species, and the only one that could be called attractive or impressive, the king vulture *(Sarcoramphus papa)*, is also found in this area, but in much smaller numbers and less frequently. Additionally a very large, beautiful hawk, the crested caracara *(Polyborus plancus)*, is often seen feeding on carcasses side-by-side with the vultures. The caracara is a very adept raptor that hunts for food when no carrion is available. Locally it is called *quebrantahuesos*, meaning "bone breaker," because of its habit of carrying the bones of dead animals high into the air and dropping them on a hard surface, then descending to eat the marrow from within the shattered pieces. Possibly because of the caracara's strong talons, the vultures often yield to it in disputes over morsels of dead flesh.

The turkey vulture is the smallest of the three species and is easily distinguished by its red head, similar to that of a turkey. The black vulture has some white visible on the tips of the underside of its wings, all the rest of its body being black. Although it is nearly fifty percent heavier than its redheaded cousin, it has a slightly shorter wingspan. You can easily distinguish between these two in flight by the large amount of gray on the underside of the turkey vulture's wings. The adult king vulture is mostly white with black trim and a multicolored head splotched with red, yellow, orange, blue and purple. In many ways it resembles a condor more than a vulture. At 3½ kilograms (8 pounds), the king vulture is twice the weight of the black vulture and 2½ times the weight of the turkey vulture. The king vulture has a wing span of two meters (6½ feet). All three species have featherless heads.

The Ecotravellers' Wildlife Guide to Costa Rica, by Les Beletsky, quotes a Maya legend that tells of the vultures and how they came to be black and bald:

> "In the old days, vultures were actually handsome, white birds with feathered heads, which ate only the finest fresh meat; they had an ideal life. One day, the vulture family, out soaring in the sun, spied a feast laid out on banquet tables in a forest clearing. They swooped down and ate the splendid food. Unfortunately for the vultures, the food had been set out by nobles as an offering to the gods. The nobles schemed to punish the unknown culprits. They set out another feast in the clearing and hid behind trees with their witch doctors. When the vultures returned for another meal, the nobles and witch doctors raced out from the trees and threw magic powder on the birds. The vultures, in their panic to escape the people, flew straight up and got too close to the sun, scorching their heads, causing their feathers to fall out. In the clouds, the magic powder turned their white plumage to black. When they returned to earth, the Great Spirit ruled that for their thievery, from that day forward, vultures would eat only carrion." (A.L. Bowes 1964)

In December 2001, I flew over Corcovado National Park in a small plane with two wildlife photographers. During the hour-and-a-half flight we saw at least a dozen king vultures and very few turkey and black vultures, the latter two mostly along the beach, and the former always over the forests. This is indicative of the difference in their modes of locating carrion. The king vulture relies primarily on smell, whereas the black vulture counts entirely on sight. Apparently the turkey vulture uses a combination of both senses. The king vulture's splendid sense of smell allows it to locate carrion on the forest floor beneath the rainforest canopy. F. G. Stiles and D. H. Jansen in an article in *Costa Rican Natural History* tell of a king vulture at Corcovado National Park that located a dead sloth wrapped in a plastic bag and buried 5 centimeters (2 inches) deep in the forest floor litter. The black vultures often follow the king and turkey vultures when they descend beneath the rainforest canopy.

As I came to understand the vultures and their importance as scavengers I came to admire many of their attributes, communication being one of the most impressive. Although the black vulture may appear to be less adept at locating its food, it seems to have the best communication skills. According to Les Beletsky there is evidence indicating that communal roosting sites tend to serve as communication centers where birds exchange information about food supply. The black and turkey vultures often roost communally in groups of five or more. The king vulture is a very solitary bird that roosts alone. I have always been impressed at how fast vultures can zero in on a dead or dying animal, but years ago I had an experience that makes me think that their communication skills may be even more impressive than researchers suspect.

In 1972 my work took me weekly to Guanacaste in northwestern Costa Rica. I used to say that there wasn't a place in the entire province where you couldn't see at least one vulture in the sky. In December of that year there was a horrible earthquake in Managua, Nicaragua that killed around 14,000 people. The newspapers told of enormous flocks of vultures that descended on the city to consume the thousands of dead human bodies that the overburdened rescue workers had not yet buried. For the two weeks following the Managua earthquake I was unable to locate a single vulture anywhere in the skies of Guanacaste Province of Costa Rica. The first black silhouettes appeared in the blue skies far to the south near the outskirts of the city of Puntarenas, about 500 kilometers (311 miles) south of Managua. I can't prove that the Guanacaste vultures went to Managua, but the circumstantial evidence is very compelling. This brings up the question of how the vultures learned about the windfall of carrion over such a great distance. I don't know the answer, and I've never read anything that might give a clue.

Vultures are a common site along roadways where they feed on road kill, mostly small creatures like toads, crabs, opossums and iguanas hit by cars. They are also common around garbage dumps where they pick through the organic garbage in search of morsels of meat. They arrive soon after a dead fish or turtle washes up on the beach or baby turtle hatchlings go trudging across the sand to the sea. At Hacienda Barú when we still had horse and cattle pasture they would come quickly to the area where the tractor and mower was chopping weeds. Cattle egrets and hawks were first to show up and kill any small animal that ran out of the brush fleeing the blades of the mower. Groups of turkey vultures and black vultures arrived a little later to scavenge through the residue in search of dead rats, lizards, crabs and snakes. The crested caracara both scavenged and hunted. King vultures are seldom seen at these sites. They tend to stay over the jungle.

I once observed a group of turkey vultures trying to retrieve an opossum from the high-voltage electrical lines where it had been electrocuted the previous night. The large black birds' feet weren't designed for perching on electrical cables, and their awkward attempts to balance on the swaying lines and grab the opossum, whose tail was wrapped around and baked to the electrical cable, reached the point of hilarity. Finally one lucky bird managed to tear the dead body loose from the cable by the tail and fly away. The carcass turned out to be heavier than the tired vulture could carry in its beak. A few meters from the cable the dead opossum dropped to the ground and the entire group of about five turkey vultures rapidly descended to fight over the carcass. The one that had managed to get the opossum off the line had to wait on the sidelines and rest after his difficult struggle while his buddies fought over the goodies.

We've all smelled the foul odor of a rotting carcass killed along the road. Here in the tropics, putrefaction is rapid and the amount of road kill is high. Can you imagine what the roadside would smell like if the vultures weren't around to play their role as cleanup crew? What the beach would smell like if the dead fish just lay there and rotted? As disgusting as the vultures' habits may seem to us, they have a key role in nature's scheme of things, cleaning up the rotting flesh and recycling it back into the ecosystem. The acid in their digestive system is so powerful that no bacteria can survive the trip through the vulture's stomach and intestines. This allows them to eat things that would kill a human and make many carnivores sick. It has even been said that the acid in a vulture's stomach will dissolve a fish hook.

Is Chepo's statement that, "Nothing will eat them, not even the ants" true? I don't know, but I've never seen anything eat a vulture's carcass. Whenever I check on one a day after it dies I always find it to be partially dried out with a slight smell than isn't quite as bad as most of what the vulture eats. In a week there won't be anything left but feathers. I've never seen ants eating them, but something does. Maybe it's only bacteria. If any of you readers know I'd like to hear from you. ❧

Chapter 29

Burgers versus Biodiversity in the Mangrove

I first heard about mangroves in the early 1970s when I was still in the cattle business. Another cattleman told me, "They're worthless swamps, no good for anything." He also told me that he had discovered a type of pasture called German grass that would invade the mangroves and dry them up. My second impression of mangrove swamps came from a lady with a similar opinion. "The mangrove is so ugly," she exclaimed, "the government should just cut down the trees, drain the swamp and fill it all in with earth. Then there would be enough room so everyone could have a nice weekend cabin near the beach." Based on these two opinions, I was prepared for something horrible when I first visited Hacienda Barú in February of 1972. At that time I had never seen a mangrove swamp and my mental image of one was vague. Reality, of course, is often quite different from our preconceived ideas. In the case of mangroves, what I saw and experienced was so diametrically opposed to what I had been told that I wondered if I might be looking at something else. The experience turned out to be a catalyst that sparked a lifelong fascination with one of the most complex ecosystems on our planet.

The mangrove estuary at Hacienda Barú is a shallow channel

that flows inland from the Barú River mouth, parallel to the beach for more than a kilometer (nearly two-thirds of a mile). Since the entrance to the channel begins near the sea, it is affected by tides. As the tide rises, salt water flows into the Barú River where it collides and mixes with the fresh water coming downstream. This, of course, causes the water to rise even further and, when it reaches a certain level, this mixture, called brackish water, flows into the estuary. The amount depends both on the height of the tide and volume of flow in the Barú River. As the tide recedes, the water level drops, and the brackish water in the estuary reverses its flow, returning to the river mouth and out to sea. Some of the brackish water remains permanently trapped in low spots in the estuary. This is the habitat where the salt-tolerant tree called mangrove thrives.

In 1972, when I first began raising cattle on Hacienda Barú, I went to see the mangrove. Armed with the knowledge that German grass would turn this "useless swamp" into a thriving pasture, I wanted to see it firsthand. The possibility of converting 20 hectares (49 acres) of "unproductive wetland" into profit-generating cattle pasture was foremost in my mind. Arriving at the estuary on horseback, we were greeted by the joyous chatter of a troop of white-faced capuchin monkeys feeding in a strangler fig tree, the first wild monkeys I had ever seen. In less than an hour we saw a spectacled caiman, boat-billed herons, a coati, a tree boa and several green iguanas. I was hooked. Never again would I entertain the idea of converting this bubbling caldron of life into a cattle pasture. The thought simply disappeared from my mind. That day I began a journey of discovery that, over the next twenty years, transformed me from a cattleman into a naturalist and environmentalist. That journey has yet to end, and I doubt if it ever will.

Five species of mangrove are found in the swamp at the Barú River estuary, but curiously, none of the five are related to each other. Common to all is a tolerance for salt and an affinity for wet, silty conditions. The five species differ in form, color, root structure and leaves. Some are very high in a chemical called tannin and have been traditionally exploited by the leather-tanning industry. Others have, in the past, been used for lumber and charcoal. Today all are protected because of the vital role they play in erosion control and habitat for countless species of marine life. Some of the species most important to commercial fishermen require the mangrove swamp environment, directly or indirectly, during part of their life cycle.

Red mangrove *(Rhizophora mangle)*, the most common species, seldom exceeds 10 meters (33 feet) in height, grows in several meters of water most of the year and has as much branching in its underwater roots as in the crown. At Hacienda Barú National Wildlife Refuge many species of birds roost and nest there, including boat-billed herons, cattle egrets, green-backed herons, neotropical cormorants, anhingas and white ibis. Others, such as the snowy egrets, great blue herons, chestnut-bellied herons, roseate spoonbills and wood storks merely visit at certain times of year. Barnacles, sponges, coral and oysters colonize the roots and are fed upon by the fish, clams, shrimp, crabs and lobsters that thrive in the water amongst the tangled mass of mangrove roots. The bottom of the estuary is an organic soup, a thick mixture of silt, decaying vegetable matter and bird guano that supports a wide spectrum of microorganisms which play an important and little-understood role in the complex realm of mangrove ecology.

Both the spectacled caiman *(Caiman crocodilus)* and the American crocodile *(Crocodylus acutus)* lurk in the dark waters beneath the trees. The larger and more aggressive crocodile generally controls the lucrative territory around the nesting site of the waterbirds and quickly gobbles up any unfortunate nestling or fledgling that falls from its nest. Iguanas that occasionally fall from the overhanging branches of the mangrove trees may also become supper for the crocodilians. Both the caiman and crocodile find the thick, inhospitable vegetation in and around the mangrove to be an ideally protected location for their own nests and reproduction.

Black mangrove *(Avicena bicolor)* thrives in the mud at water's edge and is known for the pencil-like, air-breathing roots that sprout up like an extremely coarse shag rug, covering the surface around the base of the tree. The thick trunks and branches are often hollow and provide shelter and nesting nooks for wildlife. At Hacienda Barú we often find black-headed vultures incubating their eggs there. Both green and black iguanas hide in the hollows, frequent the branches of *Avicena* and may often be seen sunning themselves in the crown.

Three other species of mangrove are present in the Hacienda Barú estuary including the rare buttonwood mangrove *(Conocarpus erectus)*, tea mangrove *(Pelliciera rhizophorae)* and white mangrove *(Laguncularia racemosa)*, the latter of which used to be exploited for its tall, straight trunk that is ideal for pole construction.

One denizen of this captivating environment, the mangrove tree crab *(Aratus pisonii)*, is of particular interest. It lives in the tops of mangrove trees, especially red mangrove, and eats mangrove leaves and large insects. Flocks of several types of egrets and herons descend into the tops of trees to prey on these small crustaceans, thus creating general panic. Some of the fleeing crabs run down the trunk, but others leap from tree to tree, and many fall into the water, only to be gobbled up by the waiting jaws of hungry fish. A general feeding frenzy ensues for both birds and fish. Fishermen often take advantage of these situations, knowing that if they throw a baited hook into the water in the midst of this confusion, it will be taken almost instantly by a crazed fish with a momentarily lowered threshold of wariness. Local fishermen refer to this phenomenon as a *garzeria*, derived from the word *garza*, the local name for the egrets and herons that start the commotion. Groups of feeding white-faced capuchin monkeys also create panic in the mangrove tree crab population and can precipitate a similar chaotic feeding situation. I don't know if the monkeys actually eat the crabs or simply dislodge them.

Along the edge of the Hacienda Barú National Wildlife Refuge estuary we have erected a stilted bird blind over the water. It is located near a roosting and nesting site for wetland birds of all kinds. At the 2004 Christmas bird count, Audubon Club ornithologists watching from the bird blind counted over a thousand waterbirds representing twelve different species, as they flew in to roost. The event begins as the sun sets. The boat-billed heron, a nocturnal feeder, flies out to forage while the many diurnal feeders come in for the night. Flocks of fifty or more individuals drop out of the sky, flare their wings and settle into the mangrove trees. For protection from predators the birds prefer islands of trees that are completely surrounded by water, and competition for space at the safest sites within the rookery can erupt into a cacophony of squawks and squabbles. The experience is truly unforgettable.

I once decided to get up before daylight and go to the bird blind for the morning activity when the majority of the birds fly away to feed. The event wasn't nearly as riotous as the dusk activity, but, as is often the case when observing tropical nature, I was rewarded with something different. As the first rays of the rising sun diluted the blackness of night I became aware of a shadow moving through

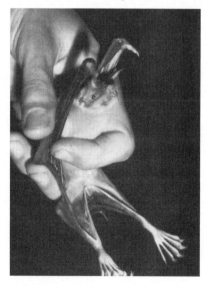

the air from one side of the open water to another. After a few minutes I caught a glimpse of the reflection from the ripples where the shadow lightly broke the

A fishing bat, sometimes called the bulldog bat. *Photo by Otto Helversen.*

glassy surface. As darkness steadily retreated, the shadow transformed into a winged hunter snatching small surface-feeding fish from the water. At some point the light became too strong for its sensitive eyes and the greater bulldog bat *(Noctilio leporinus)* made its final swoop across the swamp and flew away to the darkness of its roost.

As daylight spilled into the protected hollow of mangrove the familiar shapes of the place emerged. A southern river otter swimming near the surface of the inky black water dove beneath the surface for a minute and emerged on the bank with a crab, which it promptly dismembered, picking out the juicy flesh within. On top of a log, three large dome-shaped profiles of river turtles came into focus at the same time as the first of the boat-billed herons flew in to roost. Over the next half-hour the nighttime inhabitants of the rookery flew off to feed, mostly in silence, and the spectacle was over. But the never-ending interactions of life in the mangrove continued. I pondered the vastness of life on our planet and marveled at the wonder of this incredibly diverse habitat which supports untold thousands of species and millions of individuals. I thanked the powers that be for giving me the insight that kept me from destroying it and replacing it with a single species of plant for consumption by a single species of hoofed mammal, which in turn, would be slaughtered for the exclusive consumption of humans and their pets. ∽

And the Cards Came Tumbling Down

I had always heard of building a stack of cards but had never seen it done. So the other night I got out a deck of cards and decided to give it a try. I placed some of the cards on edge and laid others across them. The overlapping cards tied the structure together. As the stack grew, it lost stability, but the more I worked at it, the better I got. Finally, I ended up with a construction that, when viewed from the side, resembled a triangle. I was sitting there basking in my success when my wife's cat jumped on the table and down came my stack of cards.

After chasing the damn cat all over the house, until it climbed up into the rafters and sat there grooming itself with an air of disinterested arrogance, I gathered up the cards and began again. This time I was determined to build a stack that could resist a major disturbance. I found that the card pile was stronger if I made several horizontal layers, like floors in a building. I soon used up the entire deck and had to dig around in seldom used drawers and boxes to find more playing cards. The search produced five decks of cards. I went back to work, bent on building something that would resist an earthquake. My efforts produced a structure that looked a lot like a pyramid. It was quite stable and could endure minor nudges and flicks of my finger. Now I was ready for that smart-aleck cat, which of course, didn't come. My architectural marvel was still standing the next morning.

I decided to see just how strong my creation was and how much meddling it could stand. Bumping the table would make it tremble a little, but the pyramid remained standing. Slamming my fist down on the table caused one of the cards in the pinnacle to fall, but three remained holding up the top card. I returned the fallen card to its position, but now I had another idea. I studied the structure for a moment. Then I carefully removed a card from the middle of the stack. Nothing happened. The section immediately above the missing card sagged slightly, but nothing fell. I removed another card, and then another. When I slipped out the fifth card, which was near the first, the floor immediately above it drooped a couple of centimeters (an inch or so), and the next level abruptly leaned over, toppling the pinnacle in the process, but the rest of the pile held firm. After I removed another eight cards the pyramid collapsed and had to be rebuilt.

After a couple more experiments some basic principles began to emerge. It soon became apparent that the lower levels are more stable than those above them. Each individual card is more secure if it depends on several other cards for support. Cards are not all equally important, and there are always a few key pieces in the entire structure. The removal of the key cards will cause extensive damage; however, it isn't always easy to determine which ones they are.

My new diversion was turning into a learning experience. I couldn't help but think of how closely the stack of cards resembles the structure of life on earth. In the pyramid of life there are far more life forms in the lower layers than the upper ones. The simplest organisms have been around for more than three billion years and have developed a very high degree of stability and permanency. As life evolved, more layers were added. Less than one billion years ago the first simple animal forms evolved, and life moved out of the oceans onto the land. More complicated organisms such as land plants and simple animals jockeyed for their positions in the structure. Later came the arthropods such as spiders and insects, and later still the vertebrates, including reptiles, birds and mammals. Each layer in the pyramid has fewer species than the layers beneath it.

The pyramid of life has grown stronger over time. Weaker and less-adaptable species and families have perished and have been replaced by others that are fitter and better able to fill their niche in the system. Each time a damaged portion is rebuilt it is stronger than before. The disappearance of one species may not cause a major collapse but could cause changes in the structure; more damage will be done to the whole system if many other species depended on the one that disappeared. The elimination of a species will tend to affect the higher levels of the pyramid more than the lower ones.

With my card experiments, I found that when just the right key card was removed most of the structure collapsed. This event was always sudden; nevertheless, there was previous minor damage that warned of the future catastrophe. Only a really major disturbance like tipping the table at a steep angle, dropping a basketball on the pile or setting the cards on fire would destroy the lowest layers.

Since our planet is home to so many species that have been around for a long time, the pyramid of life is very strong and resistant to disturbance. Nevertheless, it has from time to time experienced some catastrophic events that severely damaged it. Scientists have determined that there have been five mass extinctions since the beginning of life on earth. The first happened over 400 million years ago, the last a mere 65 million years ago. The causes of these collapses are not clear, but evidence seems to indicate drastic changes in the planet to which many life forms couldn't adapt. The most recent was possibly due to the impact of a huge asteroid. This would be comparable to throwing a ping-pong ball at my stack of cards. Most of the upper layers would topple, and most of the lower layers would hold steady. Each extinction can be compared to a partial collapse of the pyramid of cards.

And then, along came *Homo sapiens*. In the mere speck of geological time since our first ancestors appeared on earth, humans have learned to dominate the biosphere and its millions of species. According to noted biologist Edward O. Wilson, in his landmark work, *The Diversity of Life*: "Our species appropriates between twenty and forty percent of the solar energy captured in organic material by land plants." Our superior intellect has given us such an ecological edge over other life forms that we are able to subvert them, convert the environment to our own use and even eliminate entire species. Our dominion over nature is usurping a high percentage of the natural resources on the planet and thereby destroying other living things that depend on those same resources.

In the past humans and their activities have eliminated many large animals from the face of the earth, including mammoths, mastodons, giant deer, giant bison, giant sloths, the dodo and hundreds of other species. Soon the rhinos, tigers, pandas, harpy eagles, red-backed squirrel monkeys and many others may also disappear. These life forms are high up on the pyramid, and their disappearance hasn't caused a major impact on lower levels in the past and isn't likely to in the future. But now our activities are having a more profound effect. Habitat destruction, contamination with chemicals and waste, depletion of the protective covering in the stratosphere and global warming are damaging and destroying entire ecosystems. The tall-grass prairies, tropical dry forests, tropical rainforests and coral reefs are all either gone or diminishing at an alarming rate. Species are becoming extinct even before we discover and name them. The pyramid of life is beginning to sag.

Our present situation reminds me of the delicate relationship between a parasite and its host. If the parasite kills the host, both will perish. With humans the host is the entire biosphere, with all the life forms it contains. In *The Sixth Extinction*, author Richard Leakey estimates that during the periods between the five mass extinctions, normal background extinction occurred at the rate of one species every four years. He figures that by the mid-1990s about 30,000 extinctions were occurring on the earth annually:

"Extinction at the rate of 33,000 a year, therefore, is elevated 120,000 times above background. This is easily comparable with the Big Five biological crises of geological history, except that this one is not being caused by global temperature change, regression of sea level or asteroid impact. It is being caused by one of Earth's inhabitants. *Homo sapiens* is poised to become the greatest catastrophic agent since a giant asteroid collided with the Earth sixty-five million years ago, wiping out half the world's species in a geological instant."

Can we continue to destroy our environment to the point that the upper layers of the pyramid of life drop abruptly and topple like the stack of cards? Although the analogy between the pile of cards and the pyramid of life may not be perfect, I believe there is one rule that always holds true for both. Whether eliminating cards or species, it takes a while for the pyramid to experience a collapse. With the cards the first to fall were the pinnacle, the ones at the very top. Who do you think occupies the pinnacle in the pyramid of life?

So we have a choice: to continue living as we are and risk suffering the same fate as the parasite that kills its host, or to go to work to restore the damage caused by past mistakes and learn to live in harmony with nature.

What can you do as an individual? There are lots of people working to restore the planet and teach others to value natural systems. There are many environmental organizations, each of which works in its own particular way. Some are interested in wildlife and others in entire ecosystems. Almost all of them are doing good work. It doesn't make any difference which one; pick the organization that most appeals to you and go to work.

Additionally, you can inform yourself and then inform others. There are many periodicals and books available to those interested in learning more about their environment. You could start with the two books mentioned in this article. *World Watch* Magazine is an excellent bimonthly with a wealth of information. Also from World Watch is the annual report entitled *State of the World*. This is available from the Web site *www.worldwatch.org*.

I want to leave you with a final thought from Paul Hawken, author of *The Ecology of Commerce*:

> "Underlying all ecological science is the inevitable fact that, given a chance, the earth will eventually restore itself. The salient question we need to discuss in our communities and businesses is whether humankind will participate in that restoration or be condemned by our ignorance to vanish from the planet." ∾

Chapter 31

The Pizote and the Lion

The fallen leaves were dry. Crackling sounds of animal movements were clearly audible. Something was walking 20 meters (66 feet) below the ridgeline trail where I was hiking, but the rainforest foliage shrouded its form. Although I didn't know what it was, I wasn't concerned. Few animals in the Costa Rican rainforest present a threat to people. As I continued several hundred meters down the trail, the crunching leaves seemed to follow me, always remaining about 20 meters off to the left, paralleling my path. *What could be so interested in me?* My imagination struggled to escape its normal bounds, at first lightly nudging and later dominating my senses. Most rainforest animals tend to avoid humans, not track them. An eerie feeling of being stalked seeped into my being like a light rain trickling through the thick jungle foliage. Turning my head from side to side, listening, looking, muscles and nerves tensed, I continued walking. I stopped…nothing…silence… forward ten more meters…stop…silence. I let out my breath and started forward, ashamed of my fear, determined to keep it to myself. Suddenly the leaves rustled a meter (a little over 3 feet) behind me; a twig cracked. Whirling around I caught a glimpse of the first furry bundle hurtling across the trail, then another. More sounds from the other side. I whirled back to see another dark form whiz past. The next one collided with my leg, rebounded, stumbled and took off across the trail. A quick look told me that it was a juvenile coati. I counted sixteen of the long-nosed, loop-tailed members of the raccoon family in their headlong rush across the trail, but I'm sure there were others that I didn't see. When the stampede was over and my heart slowed down to a normal beat, I was able to reflect on the event.

The group of coatis had been moving on a trajectory that would have taken them across the trail, but they encountered an obstacle, me. Not wanting to confront a human, they tried to get around me, but unwittingly walked in the same direction and found me moving with them, blocking their passage. Each step took them farther from their intended destination until near panic caused them to bolt across the trail, about half the group crossing in front and half behind me. Once across the trail the large group of females and young moved back the way they had come.

Called *pizote* locally, white-nosed coatis *(Nasua narica)* are found in groups like the one that I encountered and sometimes numbering more than thirty individuals. Juvenile males are tolerated in the troop until about two years of age when they leave to lead the solitary life of a male. Young males from the same troop may travel together for a short time but soon venture off on their own. Dominant males will return to the group during the mating season, when mature females are in heat and receptive to male company.

Closely related to *pizotes* are the raccoons, olingos and kinkajous, the former being both terrestrial and arboreal like the *pizote* and the latter two found strictly in the treetops. All of these mammals are about the same size, all are omnivorous and all belong to the *Procnid* family. Coatis dig with strong claws and rip apart rotten logs in search of grubs, insects and small lizards. Those powerful claws serve other purposes, too. Hacienda Barú guide Juan Ramón Segura says that when a dog takes chase, a *pizote* will immediately roll over on its back, feigning injury and inviting a naive canine to attack. When the dog lunges the *pizote* bites down hard on the skin of the canine's cheek or throat, quickly works its claws into the bite wound and rips the skin, opening an ugly gash. Few dogs come back for a second bout.

Though usually seen on the ground during the day, coatis are good climbers and sleep in the treetops. Pregnant females make arboreal nests where they give birth to an average of four young. Coatis often feed in the treetops as well. Strangler fig and cecropia fruit and royal palm flowers are some of their favorites. When fruit is abundant, I have seen them feeding side by side with white-faced capuchin monkeys *(Cebus capucinus)*, but on other occasions the two species clash. Hacienda Barú guide Deiner Cascante once observed a troop of monkeys grab a lone male *pizote* in the top of a tree and throw him out of the tree. Fortunately, he fell through thick foliage that broke his fall and he landed on the ground unharmed. White-faced capuchins have also been known to kill and eat helpless coati infants too young to leave their treetop nests.

In the late 1980s some of the first groups of visitors to partake of rainforest hikes at Hacienda Barú were treated to a special coati show. Near the location where the hikers normally stopped to eat lunch was a wild papaya tree heavily laden with large, round fruit. The soft, smooth trunk was riddled with scratch marks that told a tale of numerous coatis climbing to reach the fruit. There was so much competition for the treat that the papaya was never allowed to ripen. Any fruit that began to soften was ripped open and devoured by a struggling coati clinging to the tree trunk in a precarious grasp. Soon giving in to the strain, the *pizote* would typically swivel its hind feet upward, grasp the sides of the trunk with rear claws and descend head first, leaving the fruit only partially eaten and making room for another to scramble up and take its turn. This spectacle took place daily, around lunchtime, for a couple of weeks. Then suddenly all the *pizotes* disappeared from the area, leaving the tree with plenty of wild papaya which ripened and rotted on the tree. We couldn't understand what had happened to the coatis.

Almost at the same time, the Hacienda Barú forest guard, Gregorio, came to talk to me. I still remember the look on his face, brow furrowed with concern. He told of what he presumed were claw marks on a tree trunk near the lunch site for the hiking tours. He wasn't sure what had made the marks. He said the grooves were much too high on the tree and too thick to be an ocelot or anything similar. A day or two later Gregorio took me up into the jungle to show me a paw print in some soft mud. The cat track was a little larger than my open hand. For two weeks we found scratch marks on trees and terrestrial wildlife became scarce. Then suddenly everything went back to normal. The pizotes all returned as if nothing had happened. A few days later a neighbor, several kilometers away, reported having seen a mature male puma *(Puma concolor)*, sometimes called a cougar. The large feline continued to visit Hacienda Barú twice each year, in March and October. Later we put all the pieces of the puzzle together and realized that the puma's visits coincided with the times of year when there are lots of wild pigs, called collared peccary *(Tayassu tajacu)*, in our area.

Pumas tend to follow and prey on the herds of peccary that migrate around the region, but they eat other animals too. Coatis are often killed and eaten by both the jaguar *(Pantera onca)* and the puma, the two largest cats in Costa Rica. The coati's bite-and-rip technique used with dogs is useless with these carnivores. Few other creatures are a threat to pizotes, not even humans. Coati meat is edible, but not very tasty and, unless large groups of them are damaging cornfields, which they often do with great relish, humans usually leave them alone. In the absence of large felines, pizote populations can get out of control to the point that the imbalance can cause serious damage to other species.

An example is the situation on Barro Colorado Island that I

talked about in Chapter 9. When the Panama Canal was constructed in the early part of the 1900s the island was isolated in the middle of Gatun Lake. Within a couple of decades the jaguars and pumas all swam to the mainland, leaving the rich tropical forest on the island without any large carnivores, and coati numbers skyrocketed. Raccoons and coatis are classified by biologists as opportunistic predators. They normally prey on grubs, large insects and abundant small vertebrates like little lizards, but they will raid bird nests when the opportunity arises, eating the eggs or nestlings. The elevated populations of coatis and raccoons caused the demise of many species of birds on Barro Colorado Island.

Other species are affected by excessive numbers of coatis. At nesting time green iguana *(Iguana iguana)* females dig elaborate tunnels where they lay their eggs. Raccoons, coatis and domestic dogs, all strong diggers, are the primary predators of iguana nests. Too many of any or all of these predators can seriously affect populations of the long green lizards. The same is true of marine turtle nests. At Hacienda Barú we have carried out a project for the rescue of the Olive Ridley marine turtle since the mid-1980s. This involves creating a protected hatchery. Turtle eggs are recovered from natural nests before poachers can get to them and are transplanted to the nursery, where they are incubated. The most perplexing problem with these hatcheries has been keeping the raccoons and coatis out of them. We finally solved the problem by fencing the area with old roofing tin, which the *Procnids* can't climb.

In the rainy season of 2001 a herpetologist (reptile and amphibian specialist) named Mason Ryan from New York was residing at Hacienda Barú National Wildlife Refuge while carrying out a study of frogs. His work involved a lot of wandering around at night in the jungle. One day he remarked that he had found some puma scat in a particular location. The cat feces was full of what appeared to be peccary hair. A couple of nights later he returned to the same area. Mason heard a puma he estimates was 10 meters

(33 feet) uphill from him. He is sure it was a puma because of its vocalizations: a low-volume, high-pitched screech (pumas don't roar). This put him on alert, but shortly thereafter he heard another screech a few meters downhill. He believes there was a cat on each side. This is the only time during Mason's stay when he became frightened enough to stop searching for frogs and snakes and return home. He is certain that pumas were the source of the sounds, having worked as a volunteer in the Bronx Zoo cleaning the puma cages and listening to their cat sounds daily. The day after Mason's scare, guide Juan Ramón visited the area and saw a group of about a dozen collared peccary. The rain had washed away any puma tracks that might have corroborated Mason's experience. Nevertheless, a few months later a neighbor reported sighting a puma cub, a clear indication of the presence of a mated pair. This news is an encouraging sign that the ecosystem around Hacienda Barú National Wildlife Refuge is in excellent condition.

You may have felt a twinge of sadness or indignation when you read about monkeys killing baby coatis, pumas killing mature coatis or coatis killing baby birds or eating iguana and turtle eggs. Nature, however, knows no bad nor good. Everything simply is. Every living thing must eat, or die. All animal food comes from other life forms. Nature is an intricate matrix of checks and balances in which food is intertwined with population and genes. An abundance of prey attracts predators. The least fit die first. More genes get passed on from female coatis that do a good job of hiding their nests and from those that forsake the papaya treat when danger lurks. Try to observe nature, not judge its players. It makes more sense that way. ༑

Chapter 32

Strange Things Are
Happening in the Tree Tops

He wasn't supposed to do it. I was sure that Dorothy was mistaken, because that kind of thing just doesn't happen. As a matter of fact it completely cramped my style and ruined the story I had already begun. But let me back up a bit and explain.

Dorothy, Bill and I were up about as high as a twelve-story building on a platform suspended in the crown of an enormous rainforest tree called a *camarón (Licania operculipetala)*. We were observing a male three-toed sloth *(Bradypus variegatus)* that was hanging from the upper branches of another tree about 40 meters (130 feet) away. We knew for sure that it was a male, because its back was turned toward us, and we could see the swath of short hair and the wide black stripe between his shoulders, this feature being absent in females. Dorothy was watching him with her binoculars while Bill waited his turn, and I was talking about sloths. I was just getting to the part about the strange toilet habits of the three-toed sloth who, for some unknown reason, always descends to the ground to urinate and defecate. I must admit that parts of that last statement are arguable, namely the words "unknown" and "always."

The doubt surrounding "always" is easier to deal with, so let's take that first. The reason I said that the three-toed sloth *always* comes to the ground to urinate and defecate is because I had never seen a sloth defecate from the canopy, none of the other guides at Hacienda Barú National Wildlife Refuge had ever seen a sloth defecate from the canopy, and every biological text I have ever read says the sloth comes to the ground to urinate and defecate. Nowhere have I ever read or heard anything that would indicate that sloths ever defecate from the canopy.

So just at that moment Dorothy, looking through her binoculars says, "Oh look, he pooped."

I opened my mouth with the intention of blurting out some idiocy such as, *That's not possible.* But instead, thanks to the powers that be, I shut my mouth and raised my binoculars to my eyes just in time to see a second black mass fly out of the back end of the sloth.

"Oh, look!" exclaimed Dorothy, "he did it again."

I kept watching for a long time in hopes of observing this miracle again, but two quick blasts had apparently cleared the sloth's lower intestines. Eventually, I lowered my binoculars and pondered the situation. I even explained the reasons for my confusion to Dorothy and Bill. We had just witnessed an extraordinary event. I later consulted with all six of Hacienda Barú's naturalist guides. None had ever seen a sloth defecate from the canopy. I searched through books such as: *Costa Rican Natural History, Neotropical Rainforest Mammals,* and *Mammals of Costa Rica.* None mentioned any exceptions to the normal toilet behavior of the three-toed sloth. Finally I consulted a couple of biologist friends, experts on mammals, neither of whom had ever seen a sloth defecate from the canopy. Yet the fact remains that Dorothy, Bill and I clearly observed this aberrant act, and from that moment forward, I desisted from using the word "always," when referring to the sloth's weekly habit of coming to the ground to do its stuff. Since I have seen them defecate on the ground at least fifty times and only seen it once from the canopy, I will have to say "almost always" from now on.

"So," you ask, "why did you say that the sloth comes to the ground to urinate and defecate for 'unknown reasons'? Doesn't anybody have a theory that explains why?"

Oh yes, theories abound. They come in many different shapes and sizes. They go from the absurd to the barely plausible. A couple are even possible. But before we look at the theories it is important to understand a few of the basics about sloths. First, the sloth is relatively safe when it is up in the canopy. Not many predators can harm an adult three-toed sloth while it is up there. Its predators would be limited to ocelots and tayras—black weasel-like animals weighing about 6 kilograms (13 pounds). When it descends to the ground, however, it is vulnerable to many other predators including coyotes, peccaries, pumas, domestic dogs, snakes, etc. Additionally it must expend a lot of energy climbing to the ground and back up to the canopy. Any theory that attempts to explain the reasons for the sloth's toilet habits must explain what advantage the sloth gains from this behavior, and that advantage must outweigh the increased risk and energy expenditure involved in climbing to the ground and returning to the canopy. With that in mind, let's have a look at some of the different theories.

The most ridiculous I have ever heard came from a biologist guide who was leading a group of British birdwatchers. Upon spotting a three-toed sloth in the top of a tree, he explained to his visitors that the sloth comes to the ground to go to the toilet because it hangs upside down in the trees, and if it defecated from the treetops it would get poop all over itself. I held my tongue because it wasn't my place to speak up. He was in charge of the group, and I had no right to dispute his ideas in front of his clients. The flaw in his explanation is obvious. I have seen lots of sloths come down the tree to defecate, and not one came down head first. I have often photographed them holding onto a tree trunk in a vertical position with the rectum pointing downward.

The second theory is the most widely accepted, a fact which

never ceases to amaze me. This one says that by depositing its urine and dung at the base of the tree, the sloth is fertilizing its favorite trees. Sloths are classified as folivores, meaning they eat only leaves. This theory says that the sloth's bodily wastes deposited at the base of certain trees will increase the leaf production of those trees, thus benefiting the sloth. This theory reminds me of a perpetual motion machine. It would have us believe that a sloth can ingest leaves, extract all of the nutrients that are of any use to its body, expend an amount of energy equal to half a day's worth of food while at the same time doubling its vulnerability to predation, deposit the waste fiber that is left over from the digestion process under the tree, and expect to get enough extra leaf growth to make the whole ordeal worth the trouble. What's more, we are expected to believe that by making a hole with its stub tail at the base of the tree and depositing the dung and urine there, the fertilization value will be higher than if the corporal waste falls from above and is scattered over a larger area underneath the tree. My granddad was a dirt farmer with no formal education, but he knew better than that.

Quite a few years ago, I came across an article in *Smithsonian* magazine (an issue from the late 1980s) that told of some U.S. diplomats living in Surinam. They had a hobby of taking care of sloths that people brought to them. The sloths were victims of habitat destruction caused by development. Part of the regimen of sloth care included bathing them every couple of weeks. According to the article, each time the sloths were sprayed with water they would defecate. The U.S. diplomats said that the local people believed that the sloth waits for a rain before defecating, in order to prevent a potential predator from locating it by the sound of the hard pellets of dung falling through the foliage. During a rain shower the sound would be masked by that of falling raindrops. In support of this theory I can say that at Hacienda Barú National Wildlife Refuge we see a lot more sloths coming to the ground to defecate during the dry season than we do in the rainy season. Also, the day when

Dorothy, Bill and I witnessed the canopy poop, a light rain was falling. My only problem with this theory comes down to what is lost and what is gained. Although the act of coming to the ground would avoid alerting predators with the sound of falling feces, the sloth's very movement and its trip to the ground would make it more visible and vulnerable to other natural enemies. It seems that this would cancel any benefit gained by avoiding the sound of falling dung.

Another theory says that the habit of coming to the ground to defecate is a genetic memory that escaped being weeded out by natural selection. Sloths evolved several million years ago as terrestrial mammals. All of the species of giant ground sloths became extinct shortly after the end of the last ice age. Today's two-toed and three-toed tree sloths, both raccoon-size arboreal mammals, diverged genetically from the ground sloths and came to live almost exclusively in trees. Since this has happened fairly recently in evolutionary terms, the genetic memory of urinating and defecating on the ground hasn't yet been selected out. I must agree that this theory is a real possibility.

Now it's my turn. I would like to throw my own hypothesis into the ring. I say hypothesis rather than theory because a theory must include some scientific study that has produced supporting evidence. My idea has none. Instead it is a mixture of common sense, logic and a gut feeling, but, for what it's worth, here it is.

Sloths have thick coats of hair that harbor many insects, primarily mites, beetles and moths. One researcher on Barro Colorado Island in Panama counted over 800 beetles on a single three-toed sloth. Among these insects there is a particular moth, which we will call the "sloth moth." The sloth moth leaves the sloth while it is urinating and defecating in a hole at the base of a tree. The moth lays its eggs on the dung. After the eggs hatch, the larvae eat sloth dung, grow, get fat and pupate. When the time is right, a mature sloth moth emerges and promptly flies into the canopy to find a sloth.

There it lives, mates and returns to the ground to lay its eggs on sloth dung, thus perpetuating the cycle and the species.

With all that in mind, let's imagine that one day the three-toed sloth gets fed up and says; "Hey man, this is a lot of work. I'm getting tired of climbing up and down this tree just to go to the toilet. Not only that, but being on the ground scares the hell out of me. There are all kinds of nasty carnivores down there. Besides, it's no fun holding my bladder and bowel movements for a whole week. From now on, I'm gonna just let it fly from up here whenever I feel like it." What would happen to the sloth moth? It would become extinct, that's what. And that is my point. Is the sloth moth so evolutionarily naive as to trust its entire existence to the whims of a sloth? I think not. I believe that the sloth moth performs some sort of service for the sloth, something so vital that it makes the well-being of the moth a matter of survival for the sloth.

The service provided by the sloth moth is likely to be very complicated and may involve several other species. For example the moth may control the growth of algae on the sloth's hair, and this may somehow affect the population of mites. An out-of-control mite population can kill a sloth. On several occasions I have seen sloths scratch day and night for a week and then die, probably from a mange caused by rampant populations of mites. I grant that this is all pure speculation, but it makes as much sense as any other theory that has been offered. Perhaps some bright, young, ambitious biology student will decide to dedicate his or her life to unraveling the mysteries surrounding the sloth toilet riddle. Me? I'm having too much fun just watching sloths. ༜

EPILOGUE

This year at the annual meeting of the Hacienda Barú employee's association I was invited to address the group. I decided that it would be appropriate to review the changes that have taken place over the years and how these changes have brought us all on a rather unlikely journey from a typical cattle ranch with two cowboys and a fence fixer to an internationally acclaimed wildlife refuge with over thirty employees. I was a little concerned that the narration of a history which many of the listeners had actually lived might bore them, but I was pleasantly surprised. Emotions ranging from joy to tears were evident on the faces of the people to whom I spoke, those who had worked together to create the reality of Hacienda Barú National Wildlife Refuge.

Olman, presently a carpenter, previously a tractor driver, and before that an agricultural laborer, made a thought-provoking comment: "Twenty years ago when Jack sent us to plant trees in a field where we had always grown rice, I thought he had lost his marbles," he said with a devious smile. "I remember all the neighbors made fun of us and asked if we were going to eat leaves instead of rice. But today, they're all complaining about the high price of lumber, and we have all we need. I'm proud we planted those trees. I love telling people how everything we build comes from our own plantations, and that we never use wood from natural forests. But that just goes to show what's wrong with the world," he continued seriously. "We never think any further into the future than tomorrow or next week or, at most, next year. We never look ahead twenty years. That's what sets Hacienda Barú apart."

I pondered Olman's comment. I had to agree. It seems as though the world is advancing so rapidly that thoughts of a time twenty or fifty years into the future are almost nonexistent. But perhaps even more important, we appear to have forgotten the lessons of the past. *Homo sapiens* possess the unique intellectual ability to learn from mistakes, make amends and prevent future errors of a similar nature. Unfortunately, we use this ability sparingly, especially when economical considerations are at stake. Quick profits usually take precedence over long-term stability.

My attention returned to the meeting. One of the naturalist guides was talking about our role as educators in the community and how he hopes that the younger generation will learn from our example. He mentioned that the local vocational schools had recently begun offering a field of study in ecological tourism as a regular part of the curriculum. As part of their school activity, some of the students come to Hacienda Barú to work and learn. Everyone agreed that this program will tend to promote protection of natural environments throughout the region.

Again my mind wandered, this time to thoughts of education and our visitors, so many of whom have acquired a deeper appreciation of nature during their experience at Hacienda Barú. An image filtered through my mind, of an incident that had happened a few months ago:

"Look at the size of that tree," exclaimed a visitor. "What's it called?"

"I love this tree," replied Ronald, a naturalist guide. "Look at the size of these roots. They look solid, but they're really hollow and all kinds of things live inside of them—snakes, frogs, opossums." One lady cringed at the mention of snakes. Five meters (16½ feet) out from the base of the tree, where Ronald stood, the roots were knee high. "Look how long they are," said Ronald pointing out into the jungle where the root snaked across the ground and finally disappeared into a mass of vegetation. Ronald turned back to the group. "Lumber men don't like this tree because the wood is full of hard little chunks of resin. If a chainsaw hits one, the chain breaks, or maybe the saw bounces back and hurts somebody. A long time ago, before shoes were made in factories, there were lots of cobbler shops in Costa Rica. These craftsmen carved molds or forms from this wood and polished the bottom with resin. They used the molds to shape the leather. To attach the sole, the cobbler pressed the shoe leather to the bottom of the mold and the sole to the leather. He drove a nail through the sole and the leather, but when the point hit the hard resin, it bent and came right back out through the shoe leather and lodged in the sole. Since cobblers were the only people who used the wood, people started calling it the shoemaker tree, and they still call it that."

Telling true stories is our method of teaching people about the rainforest. Though the art has mostly been lost by our culture, storytelling was once the method used to pass knowledge from one generation to the next. Tribal elders were esteemed for the wisdom retained in their memories in the form of tribal legends and passed forward through the generations by storytellers. The vital knowledge retained in the legends often originated from past lessons learned the hard way, by enduring the results of grave errors which had, at one time, brought hardship, pain and death to the tribe.

At Hacienda Barú today, we make a living introducing people to the marvelous world of the tropical forest and showing them its secrets. Unwittingly we borrowed an ancient method of transferring knowledge. I thought about the common purpose for which we strive, and how we work together to teach others about the rainforest. I reflected on Olman's comment about planning for the future and envisioned Ronald enlightening minds while telling the story of the shoemaker tree. These thoughts drifted through my consciousness intermingled with images of primitive people sitting around a fire. I looked out at the group gathered around me. My dream image cleared and the pieces meshed. There we were, seated in tribal council, discussing the way we work together to make a living, considering better ways to pass on our knowledge about the natural world and create a more enriching experience for our visitors. We have, I realized, become a tribe of storytellers.

The closing statement by the president of the association brought me back to the here and now. I expected the meeting would quickly disband, but that wasn't happening. People stood around conversing, exchanging ideas and discussing the meeting. The association's accountant, a young woman from the city, congratulated me on my talk and remarked that she had never dreamed that Hacienda Barú's history was so rich in learning and human experience.

"I don't believe I have ever seen such a dedicated group of workers," she remarked. "Look at all the happy faces. Everyone is really in to what they do."

And she was right, the faces were all smiling. They reminded me of a plaque on our kitchen wall that read:

Happiness Is In Wanting What You Have
Not In Having What You Want

I looked one more time at the faces in the room. And I knew. *Everyone here is happy, and so am I. But of course we're happy. We want what we have.*

ACKNOWLEDGMENTS

No written creation is the work of a single person, and I owe a debt of gratitude to many for their assistance in compiling this collection. Each of the essays was originally written as an article and published in one of four publications: *The Dominical News, The Dominical Current, The PZ Guide* or *Quepolandia*. I wish to thank the publishers of those periodicals, Tanya and Chris Goddard, Vanessa Lynsky, Suzanne Smith, and especially Ana Lyons and Richard Sutton for their encouragement and suggestions.

Since the essays were published over a period of three years, a number of different people assisted with editing and proof reading. My wife, Diane, read every article and said it was great, regardless of what she really thought. Others who edited the original articles include: Yemaya Maurer, Purni Wortman, Jennifer Smith, Rebecca Wyatt, Chris Lamb, Kate Lomac-MacNair and Georgie Wingfield. Diane and Georgie deserve recognition for all the tender loving care they put into illustrating the chapter headings. I am grateful for the photos contributed by Alan Olander, Ben Isenberg, Charlie Foerster, Georgie Wingfield, Mayra Bonilla, Jonathan Silverman, Deiner Cascante and Riccardo Oggioni which added color and quality to the photo album. A sincere thank you to Rex and LaVonne Ewing of PixyJack Press for their encouragement and expert advice. Without LaVonne's organizational talent and expertise in graphic design this second edition would not have happened. Amy Morgan's editing skills are responsible for that extra bit of professional polish. I am grateful to Jan Betts for the time and effort she put into the cover design. She also deserves recognition for suggesting the name *Monkeys are Made of Chocolate* after her favorite essay.

I find myself at a loss for words to adequately express my gratitude to Daniel Quinn, not only for writing the foreword, but because his writings have inspired profound changes in my perception of humanity and life on our planet. Had I never opened his book *Ishmael*, the stories recounted in *Monkeys Are Made of Chocolate* might never have been told.

RECOMMENDED READING

Bright, Chris. "Chocolate Could Bring the Forest Back," *World Watch* magazine (November/December 2001).

_____. *Life out of Bounds.* New York: W.W. Norton & Company, 1998.

Brower, David. *Let the Mountains Talk, Let the Rivers Run.* Gabriola Island BC, Canada: New Society Publishers, 2000.

Coates, Anthony, ed. *Central America, A Natural and Cultural History.* New Haven: Yale University Press, 1997.

Edwards, Hugh. *Crocodile Attack.* New York: Avon Books, 1989.

Food Production and Population Growth. 2 hours, 40 min. With Daniel Quinn and Alan Thornhill, Ph.D. New Tribal Ventures, Inc., 1998. Videocassettes (2).

Giono, Jean. *The Man Who Planted Trees.* White River Junction, Vermont: Chelsea Green Publishing, 1985.

Hawken, Paul, Amory Lovins, and L. Hunter Lovins. *Natural Capitalism.* New York: Little, Brown and Company, 1999.

Hawken, Paul. *The Ecology of Commerce.* New York: HarperCollins, 1994.

Hoyt, Erich. *The Earth Dwellers.* New York: Simon & Schuster, 1996.

Jansen, Daniel H., ed. *Costa Rican Natural History.* Chicago: University of Chicago Press, 1983.

Leaky, Richard and Roger Lewin. *The Sixth Extinction.* New York: Doubleday, 1995.

Leenders, Twan. *A Guide to Amphibians and Reptiles of Costa Rica.* Miami: Zona Tropical Publishing, 2001.

Quinn, Daniel. *Beyond Civilization.* New York: Harmony Books, 1999.

_____. *Ishmael.* New York: Bantam Books, 1992.

_____. *My Ishmael.* New York: Bantam Books, 1997.

_____. *The Story of B.* New York: Bantam Books, 1996.

Terbrough, John. *Requiem for Nature.* Washington, D.C.: Island Press / Shearwater Books, 1999.

The State of the World 2003. World Watch. *www.worldwatch.com.*

Wilson, E. O. *The Future of Life.* New York and Toronto: Random House, 2002.

_____. *The Diversity of Life.* Cambridge, Massachusetts: Harvard University Press, 1992.

World Watch magazine. World Watch. *www.worldwatch.com.*

MEET THE AUTHOR

Jack Ewing's love affair with the rainforest began in 1970 when, in search of new opportunities for plying his Bachelor of Science degree and his skills as a cattle rancher, he left his native Colorado and moved his wife, Diane, and their young family to the jungles of Costa Rica. His ever-growing fascination with the rainforest, however, soon prompted his transformation into environmentalist and naturalist.

A natural-born storyteller, Jack's articles about life in the rainforest appear regularly in Costa Rican publications, and he often speaks to environmental, student and ecological traveler groups. He is currently president of two environmental organizations, ASANA and FUNDANTA. His expertise on biological corridor projects is much sought after.

"What we must do to save the rainforest," says Jack, "is connect the parks, refuges and reserves with biological corridors and then teach the people how to make a living from these natural areas without damaging or destroying them. If we want conservation to work, we have to make it profitable."

Jack and Diane live on internationally acclaimed Hacienda Barú National Wildlife Refuge where he currently serves as the director. He can be contacted by emailing *info@haciendabaru.com.*

Hacienda Barú National Wildlife Refuge is located on Costa Rica's Southern Pacific Coast—a region of distinct natural beauty, where forest covered mountains rise up from the dramatic Pacific coastline. A fantastic variety of habitats, from wetland and secondary forest in the lowlands to primary forest on the highland coastal ridge can be found on 330 hectares (815 acres). Seven kilometers (4½ miles) of trails and 3 kilometers (nearly 2 miles) of pristine beach are waiting to be explored, as are the orchid and butterfly gardens. Our mission is to protect the wildlife habitats of Hacienda Barú, while educating our visitors about its biological wealth.

Hacienda Barú National Wildlife Refuge
APDO 215-8000
San Isidro de El General
Costa Rica
phone: 011 (506) 2787-0003   fax: 011 (506) 2787-0057
www.haciendabaru.com

OTHER ORGANIZATIONS

ASANA - Asociación de Amigos de la Naturlaeza (Association of Friends of Nature), www.asanacr.org, phone 011 (506) 2787-0254

FUNDANTA - Fundación para el Corredor Biológico Paso de la Danta (Foundation for the Path of the Tapir Biological Corridor)

100% solar & wind powered since 1999

PIXYJACK PRESS INC

PO Box 149   Masonville, CO 80541 USA   **www.PixyJackPress.com**